First-Rate Reading™ ^Basics

Phonemic Awareness & Phonics

Grades K–1

by Starin W. Lewis

Carson-Dellosa Publishing Company, Inc. • Greensboro, North Carolina

Credits and Dedication

Project Director:

Kelly Gunzenhauser

Layout Design:

Jon Nawrocik

Inside Illustrations:

Stefano Giorgi

Cover Design:

Peggy Jackson

Cover Illustrations:

Stefano Giorgi

This book is dedicated to my former teachers, from preschool to graduate school. Without you, I would not have my love for learning. Thank you for all of your long hours, your enthusiasm, and your commitment to this field.

-S. L.

Table of Contents

Introduction

Phonemic awareness and phonics are different; phonemic awareness instruction teaches children the sounds (or phonemes) in words, while phonics instruction teaches the written representations (graphemes) of those sounds. Both forms of instruction are necessary to teach most students how to read. Phonemic awareness skills include sound identification, manipulation, and substitution.

Here is a brief definition of each phonemic awareness skill taught in this book:
- Phoneme isolation—identifying individual sounds (beginning, middle, and end) in a word
- Phoneme identification—identifying the same sound (usually the beginning or ending sound) in three or four words
- Phoneme categorization—finding the sound that is different (usually the beginning sound) in three or four words
- Phoneme blending—blending individual sounds to make a word
- Phoneme segmentation—counting the number of sounds in a word
- Basic syllabication—counting the number of sound "chunks" in a word
- Phoneme manipulation—deleting, adding, and substituting different sounds in a word

After students understand phonemic awareness, they learn that letters represent phonemes. The phonics sequence of this book begins with consonant sounds, then moves to more difficult concepts, such as consonant-vowel-consonant (CVC) words, long vowels, consonant-vowel-consonant-silent e (CVCe) words, and blends and digraphs.

Send home the reproducible Parent Letter (page 5) to reinforce phonics and phonemic awareness instruction at home. The more parents read and work with letters with their children, the more ready for further instruction their children will be.

Finally, use the Assessments (pages 6-7) to look at students' phonemic awareness and phonics levels at any time during the school year, including before instruction begins. Assessing students early in the year will help you determine areas in which they need practice. It will also help you group students by skill level, even if your preference is to group students with a range of skills. The first page of this two-page assessment tests students on phonemic awareness, and the second page assesses phonics. Depending on where students are in their reading development, you may choose to give students both assessments at once or just give them the phonemic awareness assessment at the beginning of the year, and wait to assess phonics when students are ready to begin learning written letters.

Name _____

Parent Letter

Dear Parents/Family:

Research shows that good readers are more successful in school. Reading is used in all other subjects and is critical for success in real life. It is important for your child to develop a solid reading base of phonemic awareness (sounds in words) and phonics (understanding letters that make those sounds). Following are suggestions and information about this area of instruction.

Phonemic Awareness is the ability to work with individual sounds and to hear syllables. This understanding should precede working with printed text. Help your child improve in phonemic awareness by doing the following:

- Make up and analyze rhymes. Say a word, such as *dog*, and ask your child to name words that rhyme (*log, fog, hog, frog*). Then, ask your child to name which sound in the word *dog* changes (/d/).
- Clap syllables in your child's name. For example, if your child's name is Jordan, clap once for *Jor* and once for *dan*. Teach your child how to clap other words.
- Help your child blend and separate sounds. Say the word *cat* and have him or her identify the three sounds (/k/, short /a/, /t/) in the word. Then, say the three sounds separately and have her blend them together to make a word.

Phonics skills require students to understand that the letters in the alphabet represent all of the sounds they make when speaking or reading. Help your child improve in phonics by doing the following:

- Teach the alphabet. Let your child sing the "Alphabet Song," play with magnetic letters, and trace letters in sand or try to write them.
- When you show your child a new word, point to the individual letters and ask him or her what sounds they make. Let your child sound-spell some words.
- Show your child that word families—groups of rhyming words—have the same ending letters and different beginning letters.

Using these ideas will help your child begin to enjoy reading. For more information, please feel free to contact me.

Sincerely,

_____

Phonemic Awareness

I. Phoneme Isolation: Total ___/6
Say the following words. Have the student identify the first sound in each word.

1. man   (/m/)   2. sun   (/s/)   3. fish   (/f/)
4. pig   (/p/)   5. rock   (/r/)   6. cap   (/k/)

II. Phoneme Identification: Total ___/6
Say the following words. Have the student identify the same sound in each group.

1. bat, bus, bite   (/b/)   2. goat, gate, gum   (/g/)   3. top, tack, ten   (/t/)
4. nap, neck, not   (/n/)   5. lip, lake, leaf   (/l/)   6. hat, hive, hog   (/h/)

III. Phoneme Categorization: Total ___/6
Say the following words. Ask the student which word in each group has a different beginning sound.

1. dog, fan, door   (fan)   2. jug, cat, king   (jug)   3. sail, soap, ten   (ten)
4. mop, milk, top   (top)   5. van, big, vase   (big)   6. win, pig, pot   (win)

IV. Phoneme Blending: Total ___/6
Say each sound separately. Ask the student to blend the sounds to form words.

1. /n/ long /o/ /t/   (note)   2. /s/ short /u/ /n/   (sun)   3. /b/ long /i/ /k/   (bike)
4. /p/ short /a/ /d/ (pad)   5. /r/ long /a/ /s/   (race)   6. /t/ long /e/ /m/   (team)

V. Phoneme Segmentation: Total ___/6
Say the following words. Have the student count the number of sounds in each word.

1. mice   (3)   2. goat   (3)   3. hi   (2)
4. spot   (4)   5. duck   (3)   6. flip   (4)

VI. Basic Syllabication: Total ___/6
Say the following words. Have the student count the syllables in each word.

1. bed   (1)   2. fish   (1)   3. birthday   (2)
4. moon   (1)   5. cowboy   (2)   6. dinosaur   (3)

VII. Phoneme Manipulation: Total ___/6
Say the following words. Have the student take off the beginning sound and tell you what sounds are left in each word.

1. bus   (short /u/ /s/)   2. lock   (short /o/ /k/)   3. fish   (short /i/ /sh/)
4. cat   (short /a/ /t/)   5. jet   (short /e/ /t/)   6. map   (short /a/ /p/)

Name _____

Date _____

Phonics

I. Letter Recognition:
Write the uppercase alphabet in random order on a separate piece of paper. Ask the student to identify each letter. Record the letters that are correct and incorrect.

Correct Uppercase Letters: _____ **Incorrect Uppercase Letters:** _____

Write the lowercase alphabet in random order on a separate piece of paper. Ask the student to identify each letter. Write the letters that are correct and incorrect.

Correct Lowercase Letters: _____ **Incorrect Lowercase Letters:** _____

II. Consonant Sounds:
Use the lowercase sheet from above. Point to the consonants. Ask the student to identify the sound of each consonant. Write the letter sounds that are correct and incorrect.

Correct Consonant Sounds: _____ **Incorrect Consonant Sounds:** _____

III. Short Vowel Sounds: ___/6
Write the following words on index cards. Ask the student to read each word. Write the words the student says.

1. cat _____ 2. lip _____ 3. mop _____
4. nut _____ 5. pet _____ 6. cup _____

IV. Long Vowel Sounds: ___/6
Write the following words on index cards. Ask the student to read each word. Write the words the student says.

1. tape _____ 2. bike _____ 3. cute _____
4. feet _____ 5. boat _____ 6. pail _____

V. Consonant Blends: ___/6
Write the following words on index cards. Ask the student to read each word. Write the words the student says.

1. crab _____ 2. trip _____ 3. frog _____
4. stop _____ 5. snap _____ 6. flag _____

VI. Basic Digraphs: ___/6
Write the following words on index cards. Ask the student to read each word. Write the words the student says.

1. shop _____ 2. thin _____ 3. chip _____
4. that _____ 5. ship _____ 6. chat _____

Introduction

Isolating phonemes is the earliest skill acquired for reading. Babies just learning to talk make noises, like "B-b-b," and "Zzzz," that turn into isolated phonemes. The trick to teaching this skill is helping young students realize that putting individual sounds together in a certain order creates a word. Conversely, students must learn how to say a word, such as *dog*, and isolate each sound when asked to do so ("/d/-short /o/-/g/"). These activities will help students learn the general concept of phoneme isolation as well as how to isolate particular spoken sounds. Note that you may have to adjust some words in these activities due to regional pronunciations.

First in Line

Students always want to be first in line! That desire will help them identify beginning sounds. State that a word is made up of little sounds. Small words usually have a beginning sound, a middle sound, and an ending sound, as if the sounds are in line. There is a first sound, and then others that follow. To demonstrate, select three students to form a line. Say a word with three phonemes, such as *pen*. Say the word first, then say each sound. As you say the /p/ sound, touch the first student's head. When you say the short /e/ sound, touch the middle student's head. When you say the /n/ sound, touch the last student's head. Ask, "Which sound was first in line?" Students should identify the /p/ sound. Give more words so that more students may stand in line. Next, have students listen to various words and figure out which sounds are first in line. Assign students to groups of three. (Let very young students remain in a whole group.) Have group members stand in lines. Then, say a word, such as *hat*, once. Then, say *hat* again, sound by sound (/h/, short /a/, /t/). As you say the /h/, prompt the first student in each small group to say /h/ with you. When you say the second sound (short /a/), prompt the second students to say short /a/ with you. And, when you say the final sound (/t/), prompt the last student in each line to say the /t/ sound with you. Say the entire word again and ask students to identify the first sound (/h/). Have the first student go to the end of the line. Repeat the process with a new word, such as *kid*, *fog*, *bed*, *mad*, or *run*, and with middle and ending sounds.

Center Sounds

Explain that all words have beginning sounds. Give several examples. Hold up an item from your desk, say the word, then say its beginning sound. Hold up several more items from your desk. Each time, say the word and then let students identify the beginning sound. Next, assign students to small groups. Send each group to a different classroom center. Send kindergarten students to the housekeeping center, building center, alphabet center, etc. Send first-grade students to the writing center, reading center, science center, etc. Tell each group to find a particular object in the center. Have students in each group show the object to the class, say its name, and identify its beginning sound. If students are ready, let each group member choose his own object. Be ready to explain the blend in a word like *block* if students are confused. If students are not ready for this particular skill, plant objects without blends in the centers beforehand.

Echo-o-o-o

Explain that in a cave, sounds echo, or bounce back and repeat. If someone says a word, the sound waves bounce off of the walls. It sounds like the ending of the last word spoken is being repeated. If possible, take students to a large, empty room, such as a gym, where they can shout at a wall to hear their own echoes. Say, "echo-o-o-o." Ask, "What was the ending sound of my word?" Students should respond that the last sound in the word was long /o/. Let students pretend to be an echo. Say a word and have students repeat the last sound in the word. For example, if you say the word *van*, students would repeat back /n/. If you said the word *goat*, students would repeat back /t/. Also, try other words, such as *yes, job, if, gum, car,* and *five.* Congratulate the class on being a good echo.

Classroom Stars

Remind students that all words are made of sounds. In some words, there is a beginning, middle, and ending sound. Ask, "What is the last sound you hear in the word *sun*?" Give each student a foil star sticker for identifying the /n/ sound. Have each student press the sticker into the palm of her hand. Next, sing the "Ending Sound Song" (below) to the tune of "Twinkle, Twinkle, Little Star." At the end of the song, say a word. Then, repeat the first four lines. If students know the ending sound of the word, they should raise their hands and show the star stickers. After singing, have a volunteer identify the ending sound. Repeat the song several more times, substituting words in the last two lines, such as *dig, jam, mop,* and *run.*

Song:
Can you hear the ending sound,
Of the word that I have found?

Raise your hand up in the air,
If the last sound you can hear.

(Say the word twice, slowly.) p-e-t, p-e-t
(Sing the first two verses again.)

Word Sandwich

Give each student a copy of the Word Sandwich reproducible (page 11). Tell students to color the bread slices brown and the tomatoes red, then cut out the shapes. Have each student make "word sandwiches" to isolate the middle phonemes in short words, such as *pop*. Have each student pick up a "bread slice," repeat the /p/ sound after you, and place the bread on her desk. Ask each student to pick up the "tomato," say the short /o/ sound, and place the tomato on top of the bread slice. Next, direct each student to pick up the other bread slice, say the /p/ sound again, and complete the sandwich. Ask students what sound was in the middle of their word sandwiches (short /o/). Have students make more word sandwiches with other words, such as *mom*, *bib*, *Bob*, *dad*, *did*, *pep*, and *pup*.

Sally the Search Dog

Explain that some dogs search for things and people. Help students make dog puppets that search for sounds. Give each student a copy of the Sally the Search Dog reproducible (page 12) and a paper lunch bag. Have each student color and cut out the dog parts and collar. Then, direct him to glue the ear and face pieces to the bottom of the bag, glue the paws to the middle, glue the collar onto the dog's neck, and glue the tail to the back. Let each student practice moving the puppet's mouth by placing his hand inside of the bag and opening and closing his hand. After sufficient practice, tell students that this dog's name is Sally the Search Dog, and Sally will search a word for the middle sound. Say a word. When "Sally" identifies the middle sound, have students raise their hands and move the puppets' mouths to say the middle sound. Use the words *dog*, *tail*, *nose*, *feet*, *bite*, *wag*, and *lick*. Make sure students are identifying the middle sounds and not the letters.

Word Worm

Provide three 2" (about 5 cm) circles for each student. Each student's circles should be cut from a different color of construction paper. Also, give each student a piece of green construction paper. Direct each student to glue his three circles to the green paper to make a "word worm." The three circles should be touching each other and should look like a caterpillar crawling horizontally across the paper. Have each student draw two antennae and a face on the far left circle. Explain that the word worm will help each student identify the beginning, middle, and ending sounds in a word. First, tell students whether they should listen for the beginning, middle, or ending sound of a word. Then, as you slowly say each sound in the word, direct each student to touch one of the caterpillar's circles. For the first sound, students should touch the worms' faces. During the middle sound, students should touch the middle circles. When students hear the ending sound, they should touch the last circles. Have students identify the sound you asked them to listen for. Use words such as *not*, *hat*, *dog*, *sun*, *hen*, *set*, *lap*, *pig*, and *cub*.

First-Rate Reading™: Phonemic Awareness and Phonics • CD-104018 • © Carson-Dellosa
Basics

Word Sandwich

Color the bread slices brown.
Color the tomato red. Cut out the pieces.

Sally the Search Dog

Color and cut out the pieces.
Glue them to a paper bag to make a dog puppet.

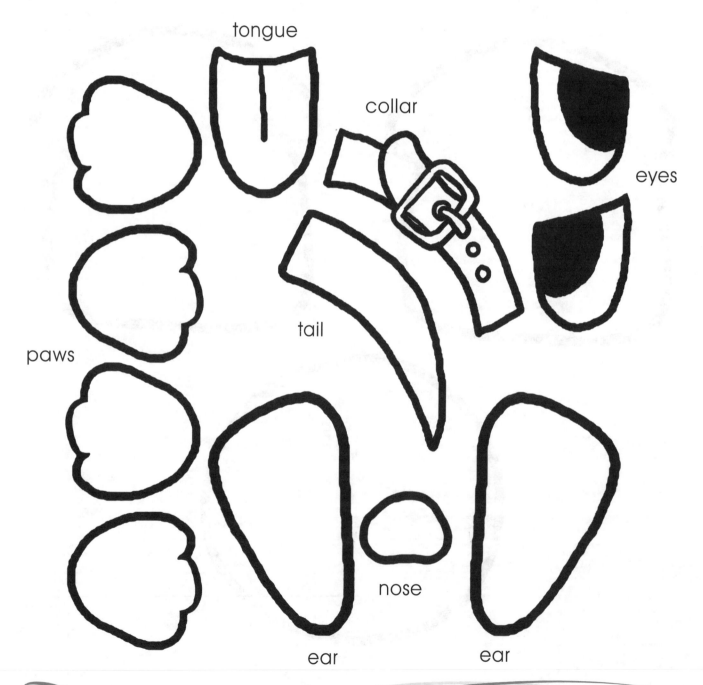

tongue

collar

eyes

paws

tail

nose

ear

ear

Phoneme Identity

Introduction

After students learn to isolate phonemes, they are ready to learn how to identify them. Identification is a simple concept: students should be able to hear that the beginning sounds in the words *fox, first, four,* and *fan* are all the same. When students learn to recognize a repeating sound, they will be ready to put that sound with a grapheme.

Sound Book

Use this lesson as an informal assessment or to practice sound identification. Draw a picture of a cat on the board. Ask, "What sound do you hear at the beginning of the word *cat?*" (Students should name the /k/ sound.) "What is another word that has the same beginning sound as *cat?*" Reinforce correct responses. When a student suggests a word that can be drawn, such as *cow,* draw a picture of the second /k/ word next to the cat. Ask, "Do these two words have the same beginning sound? What is the sound?" Give each student paper and crayons. Say, "I will say a word. Think about its beginning sound." Say the word *pig.* Ask students to identify the beginning sound but to refrain from saying the answer. Then, have each student draw a picture of another object whose name has the same beginning sound, such as a *pail, pencil,* or *pizza.* Walk around and ask students to identify their pictures. If a student has drawn a picture with an incorrect beginning sound, repeat the word and have him draw a new picture. When students are finished, have them show their pictures to the class and say the names of the drawings. Collect the pictures in a class book. Add a cover and the title *Beginning Sounds: /p/.* Repeat the lesson with different consonant sounds to create a series of sound books.

Turtle Technique

Provide a small, disposable bowl, green construction paper, glue, and scissors for each student. Tell students, "Many words have a beginning sound, a middle sound, and an ending sound. For example, what sound is at the beginning of the word *turtle?*" Pronounce the word *t-t-t-turtle* to emphasize the beginning sound. Make turtles to help students find other words that begin with the /t/ sound. Have each student cut four foot shapes from the green construction paper, a triangle for the turtle's tail, and a spade shape for the turtle's head, then glue the feet, head, and tail to the rim of the bowl (the turtle's shell). (Younger students may need precut construction paper for their turtles' parts.) Let each student draw a mouth and eyes on the turtle's head. Ask students to identify the beginning sound of *turtle* again (/t/). Have each student place his turtle next to another object that begins with the /t/ sound, such as the teacher, a table, tape, or a classmate whose name begins with the letter t. Let students share their /t/ words.

Triplets

Make two copies of the Phoneme Identity Picture Cards reproducible (page 15). Cut apart the picture cards. Remind students that you have been working on beginning sounds. Say four words: three with the same beginning sound and one with a different sound, such as *dog, doughnut, cat,* and *door.* Tell students that three of the words are triplets because there is something the same about all three of them. Ask students to identify the triplets (*dog, doughnut,* and *door*), then name the one that is different (*cat*). Challenge students with another question, such as, "Which three words have the same beginning sound: *red, safe, silly, sun?*" Students should respond that *safe, silly,* and *sun* are triplets. Give each student a picture card and say each picture's name: *leaf, fish, sun, pear, feather, wagon, snake, worm, five, ladder, pie,*

seven, wolf, pillow, lion. Tell students that the picture name on each card is part of a triplet; three classmates have pictures with the same beginning sound. When you say "Triplet!" have students walk around and try to find two other students that have pictures of objects with the same beginning sound. (There are only 15 pictures on the reproducible. Making two copies will create enough for a classroom set, but there will be duplicates, so explain that a student cannot be in a group with someone who has the same picture.) When students have found their triplets, have them share their words and similar sounds. Answer key: *feather, five, fish; ladder, leaf, lion; pear, pie, pillow; seven, snake, sun; wagon, wolf, worm.*

Phonemic Identity Puzzle

Give each student a copy of the Phoneme Identity Picture Cards reproducible (page 15) and a sentence strip. Review the names of each picture on the reproducible. (See Triplets activity, above.) Have students cut apart the pictures. Direct each student to find two pictures that have the same beginning sound, then have him find one picture that does not have the same sound. Instruct each student to glue the three pictures to the front of his sentence strip, then make a second puzzle on the back of the sentence strip using different pictures. Pair students. Have partners exchange puzzles, try to find the pictures that do not belong, and check their answers with their partners. Store the puzzles in a center for future practice. To increase the difficulty of this activity, let students draw their own picture puzzles on sentence strips and store them in the center, as well.

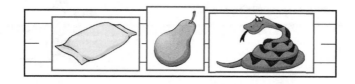

Phoneme Identity Picture Cards

Cut out the pictures. Use them for letter and sound activities.

In the Bag

Copy the Phoneme Identity Picture Cards reproducible (page 15), cut apart the cards, and laminate them. Gather five paper bags. Draw one of the following on each bag: a window, the number 6, a pig, a lemon, and the number 4. Place the cards and bags at a center. When students go to the center, have them work together to sort the pictures. Instruct students to say the name of each picture and listen for the beginning sound, then find a bag with a picture on it of something that begins with the same sound. For example, if the picture is a worm, it would go into the "window" bag. If the picture is a feather, it would go into the "4" bag. Encourage students to work together to sort the pictures.

Sound Store

Send a note home explaining that students will set up a classroom "Sound Store" to display items that start with /s/, /r/, or /n/. Ask families to help each student find one household object that starts with one of those sounds, such as a soup can, a box of raisins, or a napkin. Students may choose which sounds to represent. Have families label the items with students' names if they would like them returned, and send the items to school with students. Use masking tape to divide a large table into three sections: one for /s/, one for /r/, and one for /n/. (Or, use three small tables or desks.) Ask each student to show her item to the class, and say the item's name and its beginning sound. Next, have her place the item in the correct section. Continue sorting the Sound Store items, then ask students to repeat the names of the objects in each section. Then, mix up the items. Throughout the day, ask individual students to "shop" in the Sound Store by "purchasing" two *s* items and one *n* item, etc. Check students' purchases to ensure they gathered correct items, then return them to the table and give other students time to shop.

Sorting Socks

Give each student a copy of the Sorting Socks reproducible (page 17). Have each student think of two items he can draw that end with the same sound. For example, *bat* and *net* would be easy to draw, *not* and *tight* would not. Direct each student to draw a picture of one item on a sock and draw the other item on the other sock. (Cut large pictures from magazines for younger students to glue on the socks.) Help students cut out the socks. Have students write their names on the backs. Then, collect a sock from each student and put it in a pile. Place the second set of socks in a different pile, faceup. Give each student one sock from the first pile but do not return a sock to its original owner. Direct students to look at their socks and identify the ending sounds of the pictures. If students are unsure, have them go to the original artists and ask them to identify the pictures. Then, tell each student to look at the socks on the floor and find one that has the same ending sound. (It is fine if students don't find the matching sock that the artist originally drew, as long as the student finds a matching sound.) When students have found a matching pair, have them share their sock sounds. Attach a clothesline or heavy string to a bulletin board and use small clothespins to attach the socks. Title the board "Ending Sounds Knock Our Socks Off!"

Sorting Socks

On the socks, draw pictures
that have the same ending sounds. Cut out
the socks and use them to play a game.

Phoneme Categorization

Introduction

After students learn to hear and recognize sounds, teach them to put these sounds in categories. Students have been exposed to some of this already by completing activities that involve identifying matching sounds and additional sounds that do not belong. The following activities will help students learn to sort words according to their sounds.

Lasso It!

Give each student a piece of string or yarn approximately 18" (45 cm) long and a copy of the Phoneme Categories reproducible (page 20). Tell students the name of each picture and have them cut apart the cards. (Picture names are *pencil, kite, mug, pumpkin, bee, turtle, monkey, cake, bear, ball, moon, pig, tooth, ten, cat.*)

Ask students to find the pictures of the turtle, monkey, and moon. Explain that two pictures have the same beginning sound, and one picture does not have the same beginning sound. Explain that a *lasso* is a rope that cowboys and cowgirls use to catch animals. Have students use lassos to "catch" the different-sounding picture. First, repeat the name of each picture. Instruct students to listen carefully to the beginning sound of each word. Then, ask each student to identify the card that does not have the same beginning sound and use her string to make a circle around the odd card. She has just lassoed the different card! Have students find the pig, kite, and pumpkin cards. Repeat the picture names while students listen to the beginning sounds. This time, have each student lasso the different card without any help from the rest of the class. Share the answer with the class. Repeat the activity with other combinations.

Counter Choice

Give each student a copy of the Phoneme Categories reproducible (page 20) and three 2-colored counters or three connecting blocks (two of one color, one of a different color). Tell students the name of each picture. (See Lasso It!, left, for names.) Then, have students cut apart the cards. Work with the class to categorize different beginning sounds. Direct students to place the pictures of the cat, cake, and pencil in front of them. Tell students that two of the pictures have the same beginning sound, and one does not. Repeat each picture's name. Have students listen to the beginning of each word and identify the picture with the different beginning sound. Have each student put two counters (lighter side up) on the two pictures that have the same sound and place one counter (darker side up) on the picture with a different sound. After students have placed their counters, ask, "Which picture does not have the same beginning sound?" Repeat using different pictures.

First-Rate Reading™: Phonemic Awareness and Phonics • CD-104018 • © Carson-Dellosa
Basics

/F/oneme /F/un Card Game

Pair students and give each pair a copy of the Phoneme Categories reproducible (page 20). Review the picture names with the class. (See Lasso It!, page 18, for picture names.) Tell students to cut apart the cards. Explain that the object of the game is to collect two picture cards that begin with the same sound and one picture card that begins with a different sound. Students should place the cards facedown on the floor, mix them, then restack them. Instruct one student to deal himself and his partner three cards from the pile. Tell students to look at their cards to determine the beginning sound of each picture. Remind students that they are trying to collect two cards that start with the same sound and one card that does not. Have Player A take a card from the pile, look for a match in his hand, then discard one card. Player B should then draw a card, look for a match, and discard a card. Students should alternate turns until one player has two cards that begin with the same sound and one card that begins with a different sound. When a player has that combination, he should say "Same Sound!" and show his cards. He must then say the names of his picture cards and point out the one that is different. If students draw the entire deck and there is no winner, they should shuffle the discard pile, turn it over, and continue play.

Clap on the Different One

Play a game that requires students to be good listeners. Say three words, two of which begin with the same sound and one word that begins with a different sound. The odd word may come at the beginning, middle, or end of the list. Repeat the words a second and third time. On the third time, tell students to clap when they hear the different beginning sound. Give students an example by saying, "Happy, house, bear." Repeat the words. Ask, "Which word has a different beginning sound?" Students should name *bear* as the word with the different beginning sound. Tell the class, "This time when I say *bear*, you should clap." Say the words in the same order (*happy, house, bear*) and encourage students to clap when they hear *bear*. Give another example if necessary, then stop coaching students about which word to clap on and find out if they can hear the different sounds themselves. Repeat the process as many times as desired using other word groups, such as *van, day, dish; fog, first, goose; wash, leaf, well; yes, yarn, mop; rabbit, zebra, zoo;* and *bus, bee, nest.*

Phoneme Categories

Cut apart the picture cards. Listen
to your teacher explain how to use them.

First-Rate Reading™: Phonemic Awareness and Phonics • CD-104018 • © Carson-Dellosa
Basics

T-Shirt Time

Give each student a copy of the T-Shirt Time reproducible (page 22) and a few crayons. Explain that in each row there are three T-shirts. Each T-shirt has a picture on it. Two T-shirts in each row have pictures whose names start with the same sound. One T-shirt in each row has a picture that starts with a different sound. Tell students the name of each picture in the first row: *dog, duck, sun*. Direct students to color the T-shirt with the picture that has a different sound from the others. Repeat with the remaining rows of T-shirts, then go over the answers. (Picture names in the second row are *worm, feather, fish*. Picture names in the third row are *mouse, leaf, mop*.)

Rabbit Ears

Play a Rabbit Ears game to help students practice being excellent listeners. Explain that rabbits have very long ears and are excellent listeners. Rabbits also like to eat carrots. Explain that the object of the game is to get as many carrots as possible. Enlarge the rabbit's face pattern (right) for each student. Have each student color and cut out the rabbit face, then glue it to the end of a craft stick to make a puppet. Assign students to groups of three. Have each group think of a team name, such as the Reading Rabbits. Write each team name on the board. Say three words to a team, two that begin with the same sound and one that does not. Ask the team to work together to identify the odd word in a set amount of time. Have remaining teams also try to identify the odd word because they will be asked if they agree or disagree with the opposing team's answer. When the first team comes to a consensus, have them give an answer. Ask the other students to hold up their rabbit puppets only if they agree with the answer. If the first team is correct, give them a "carrot." (Use orange chalk to make a tally mark by their team name on the board.) If the team is not correct, identify the correct word, then repeat with the remaining teams. The "rabbits" with the most carrots at the end of the game win.

Picture Perfect

Assign students to small groups. Give each group member paper and crayons. Quietly assign a consonant sound to each group. Instruct all but one of the group members to each draw something that starts with that sound. Ask the remaining group member to draw something that does not start with the same sound. For example, if the group's letter sound is /b/, they could draw a bat, a ball, a bird, and a sun. When the drawings are complete, have one group show the pictures to the class. Let each group member say the name of his object. Then, ask the rest of the class to identify the word that begins with a different sound. Allow other groups to share pictures, as well. Create a bulletin board by stapling the groups' pictures on the board in random order. Add the title "Which Pictures Start with Different Sounds?" Let students visit the board and review which pictures start with different sounds.

T-Shirt Time

Color the shirt in each row that has
a picture with a different beginning sound.

First-Rate Reading™: Phonemic Awareness and Phonics • CD-104018 • © Carson-Dellosa
Basics

Phoneme Blending

Introduction

The multistep process of blending phonemes requires knowing how to hear them, isolate them, and identify them. It is a complex skill because students are required to take isolated sounds and combine them to make a group of sounds—a word. For example, if a student hears the sounds /k/, short /a/, and /t/, she should be able to say those sounds faster and closer together until she can identify the word *cat*. Additionally, instruction for this skill often requires students to learn to write the letters that make the sounds, then read what they have written.

Remote Control

Provide a real remote control for this activity. Explain that when students blend sounds together, they can make words. Show your remote control and explain that it can speed up or slow down a videotape playing on a television. Then, use the remote control to "slow down" your words. Click the remote in the direction of your mouth. Say each sound of the word *tag* very slowly (/t/, short /a/, /g/). Next, use the remote control to "speed up" the sounds to normal speed. Click the remote toward your mouth again. Say the sounds of the word faster each time until they clearly blend to make the word *tag*. Ask, "What word did I make?" Reinforce the concept by saying, "When I blended the sounds /t/, short /a/, and /g/, I made the word *tag*. I will say the sounds of other words in slow motion. Try to blend the sounds together and tell me the words." Say the words listed below very slowly. (Remember, you are saying sounds, not letters.) Have students blend the sounds together to form words. Words that work well for this activity are *if* (short /i/, /f/), *bus* (/b/, short /u/, /s/), *dime* (/d/, long /i/, /m/), *get* (/g/, short /e/, /t/), *lap* (/l/, short /a/, /p/), *fast* (/f/, short /a/, /s/, /t/), and *crib* (/k/, /r/, short /i/, /b/).

Linking Sounds

Explain again that words are sounds linked together. Select three students to stand in a row with their arms down. Have the first student say a /d/ sound. Tell the second student to say a short /u/ sound. Have the third student say a /k/ sound. Have the three students repeat their sounds individually. Next, have students link arms and say their sounds more quickly so that they blend. Ask the rest of the class, "What word did these three students make when they linked the sounds together?" Students should recognize the word *duck*. Repeat with different students. As students get better at hearing the sounds, assign words with more phonemes and use a larger number of students. If students have trouble with this activity, use two-phoneme words, such as *if*, *pie*, *day*, *no*, *go*, *tie*, etc.

Magic Wands, Magic Words

Provide a craft stick and several star stickers for each student. Bring in a hat for yourself. (A top hat is ideal, but any hat will work.) Have students make magic wands that will turn sounds into words. Direct students to stick the stars onto their craft sticks to make the wands. Next, bring out your "magic" hat. Say, "/h/, short /a/, /t/." As you pretend to throw each sound into the hat, have students wave their magic wands to blend the sounds and turn them into a word. As students wave their wands, repeat the sounds faster and faster until they blend into the word *hat*. Ask a volunteer to identify the word. Use the suggested words below or challenge students by using words with more sounds. Suggested Words: *cake* (/k/-long /a/-/k/), *boat* (/b/-long /o/-/t/), *pet* (/p/-short /e/-/t/), *log* (/l/-short /o/-/g/), *run* (/r/-short /u/-/n/), *swim* (/s/-/w/-short /i/-/m/), *clap* (/k/-/l/-short /a/-/p/).

Betcha Can't Blend It!

Have students play a game called Betcha Can't Blend It! Write the words *teacher* and *class* on the board. Say the sounds of a word, such as "/l/, short /o/, /k/," then say "Betcha can't blend it!" At this point, have students work together to try to blend the sounds to make the word *lock* in just 30 seconds. Call on a student to say the word. If the first student is incorrect, ask two more students. If one of them gets the word right, make a tally mark on the board under the word *class*. If they get it wrong, make a tally mark on the board under the word *teacher*. Whoever has the most points at the end of the game is the winner. (To build confidence, play several times until the class wins the challenge.) Use the following suggested word list or come up with your own. Suggested Words: *fan* /f/-short /a/-/n/, *web* /w/-short /e/-/b/, *lip* /l/-short /i/-/p/, *knot* /n/-short /o/-/t/, *hum* /h/-short /u/-/m/, *cap* /k/-short /a/-/p/, *best* /b/-short /e/-/s/-/t/, *stick* /s/-/t/-short /i/-/k/, *frog* /f/-/r/-short /o/-/g/, *dust* /d/-short /u/-/s/-/t/, *vest* /v/-short /e/-/s/-/t/, *lamp* /l/-short /a/-/m/-/p/

Blending Letter Sounds

Ahead of time, trace and cut out this combination of letters: five of the letter *t*; two each of the letters *a, e, h, i, n, o, p, s,* and *u*; and one each of the letters *b, c, d, f, g, m,* and *r*. Assign students to groups of three and have the group members sit in a row. Give each student in each group one letter of a three-letter word, such as *pat, can, red, get, sit, him, top, hot, fun,* or *bus*. Explain that each letter has a sound, and when the letters' sounds are blended together, they can make words. Direct each group member to say the sound of her letter. Have students work together to blend the sounds and form a word. Next, let each group say the sounds of their letters for the rest of the class to hear. Ask the rest of the class to blend the sounds to make a word. Confirm the correct answer with the group. Finally, let students staple the letters together and post them on a bulletin board titled "Words We Can Read."

Word Pull

Explain that taffy is a stretchy candy. To make it, people stretch it and let it shrink several times. Consider providing taffy for students to eat while you explain this activity. (Get families' permission and information about food allergies and religious or other food preferences before offering food to students.) Have students stretch words and then shrink them, like taffy. Copy the Word Pull reproducible (page 26) for each student. Note that there are four pieces of taffy on the sheet to use for words that students will stretch, shrink, then write. Start with the word *let*. Slowly say the "stretched out" sounds in the word *let* as you make a stretching motion with your hands. Tell students that the sounds will "shrink" together to make a word. Move your hands closer together as you ask students to blend the sounds of the word *let*. Then, write the letters on the board as students write them on the reproducibles. Say, "The first sound is /l/. What letter makes a /l/ sound?" Write *l* on the board. Ask, "What letter makes the short /e/ sound?" Write an *e* next to the *l*. Finally, ask, "What letter makes a /t/ sound?" Write a *t* next to the *e*. Point to each letter and blend the sounds until students hear the word *let*. Have students write *let* on the first piece of taffy. Repeat with the words *had, mom,* and *tub*. Have students cut out the taffy pieces and put them in clear, plastic cups to keep at their desks for the rest of the day, like jars of candy.

Stringing Sounds Together

Ahead of time, make one enlarged copy of the Stringing Sounds Together reproducible (page 27). Cut apart the letters. Attach a clothesline or heavy string to a bulletin board or between two tall classroom objects. Explain that words are made by "stringing together" sounds. Use small clothespins to clip the letters *b, a,* and *t* to the clothesline. Ask students to string together the sounds. Point to each letter and say the sounds /b/, short /a/, and /t/ repeatedly. Ask, "What word do these sounds make together?" Students should identify the word *bat*. Repeat with other words. Use the remaining letters to create new words.

Word Pull

As your teacher stretches and shrinks a word, write the word on a piece of taffy. Cut out the taffy.

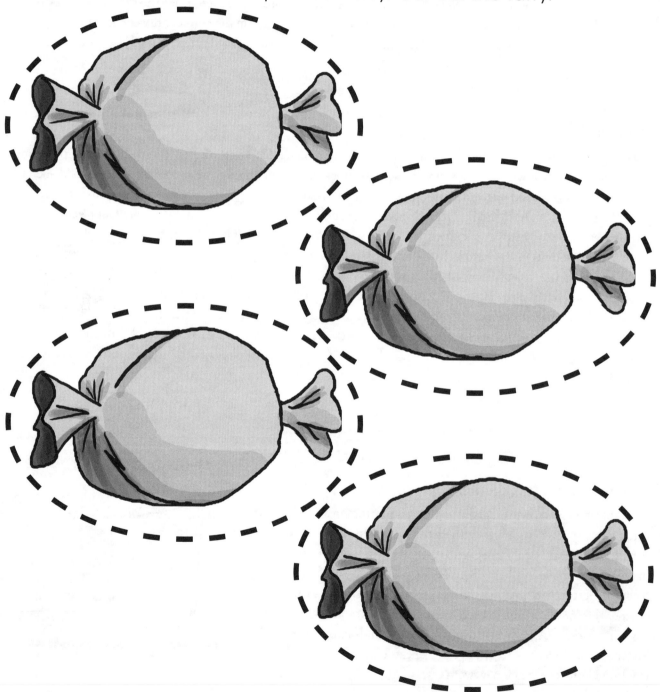

Stringing Sounds Together

Cut apart the letters. Help your teacher
clip the letters to a clothesline to build words.

a	a	b	e	e	f
f	i	i	n	n	n
o	o	p	p	s	s
s	t	t	t	u	u

Introduction

To master this skill, students simply need to be able to reverse the thought process involved in phoneme blending. They should be able to hear a word and break it apart into its individual sounds. After breaking apart a word, students should be able to count the sounds and identify each one. Unless there are blends, digraphs, or silent letters in the word, students may be able to identify the matching letters for the sounds and use the sounds to spell the word.

Slow It Down

Provide a real remote control for this activity, which is the opposite of the Remote Control activity (page 23). Explain that when students blend sounds together, they can make words. Show students the remote control and say that it can speed up or slow down a videotape playing on a television. Then, use the remote control to "slow down" your words. Say the word *bag* at regular speed, then click the remote control toward your mouth. Say the word *bag* more and more slowly until you say the sounds /b/, short /a/, and /g/. Ask, "How many sounds are in the word *bag*?" Students should be able to count three sounds. Repeat the process by saying the word *did* at regular speed. Click the remote control toward your mouth. Slow down the speed of the word until you are saying the sounds /d/, short /i/, and /d/. Have students count the number of sounds. Repeat with shorter or longer words, depending on students' skill levels. To enhance the activity, choose short action words, such as *swing, run, jump, hop,* etc. As students take turns slowing down these words, have them also mimic slowing down actions to go with the words.

Break Apart a Word

Provide six interlocking blocks for each student. Explain that students can break a word into individual sounds. For example, display a set of three interlocking blocks. Tell students that the connected blocks are like an entire word made of individual sounds (the individual blocks linked together). Say, "Let's pretend that the connected blocks are like the word *cat*. If I think about the sounds I hear in *cat*, I can hear a /k/ sound at the beginning (pull off one block), a short /a/ sound in the middle (pull off the next block), and a /t/ sound at the end. That makes three sounds in the word *cat*: /k/, short /a/, and /t/." (Show the individual blocks as you say the sounds.) Have students count the sounds in words, as well. Say one of these words with four or fewer sounds: *if (2), he (2), at (2), log (3), cup (3), dig (3), back (3), nest (4),* and *trap (4).* Direct students to connect a given number of blocks, repeat each word, and think about the number of sounds they hear in the word. Begin with shorter words and group words with the same numbers of sounds so that you do not give away the answers by telling students how many blocks to connect. Have each student pull off a block for each sound she hears in the word. Then, have students count the number of blocks. Before stating each new word, tell students to put the blocks back together.

Karate Chop

Explain that words can be "chopped" into individual sounds. For example, the word *mud* has three sounds. Make a chopping sign with your hand as you say the sounds /m/, short /u/, /d/. Ask students to chop other words into individual sounds. Say a word and show students how to make a chopping motion on their desks for every sound in the word. Explain that saying the word quietly while chopping will help them count the number of sounds in the word. Direct students to count the number of "chops" or sounds in the word. Repeat using words like *on* (2), *up* (2), *sled* (4), *wig* (3), *bat* (3), *plum* (4), *fox* (4: /f/- short /o/- /k/- / s/), and *plant* (5).

Count and Move Game

Assign students to pairs. (Groups of three or four will also work.) Give each pair an enlarged copy of the Count and Move Game Board reproducible (page 30), two game pieces (coins, counters, etc.), and two copies of the Count and Move Cards reproducible (page 31). Have students cut apart the cards and review the names of the pictures with your help. [Picture names are *sun* (3), *wagon* (5), *frog* (4), *cat* (3), *web* (3), *duck* (3), *flag* (4), *tent* (4), *gift* (4), *sock* (3), *bus* (3), *hen* (3), *crab* (4), *doll* (3), *fox* (4), and *milk* (4).] Work with students to count the number of phonemes (sounds) in each word. Have students use pencils to write the numbers on the backs of the cards. To begin the game, have one player in each pair place his picture cards faceup in a pile. Have each player place a game piece on the first space on the game board. Instruct Player A to look at the picture on the top card and say the word. If the player does not recognize the picture, he may ask the other player to identify it. Player A should count the number of sounds in the word. Let Player B lift the card and look on the back to see if Player A counted the number of sounds correctly. If Player A is correct, he should move his piece the same number of spaces as the number of sounds in the name of the picture. For example, if Player A correctly counts three sounds in the word *web*, he should move his piece three spaces. If Player A is incorrect, he should move no spaces and place the card at the bottom of the pile, and Player B should take a turn. Have players alternate turns until one reaches the end and wins. A player does not have to draw a card with the exact number of sounds as there are spaces remaining in order to win the game.

Count and Move Game Board

Use the game board
with the Count and Move game.

First-Rate Reading™: Phonemic Awareness and Phonics • CD-104018 • © Carson-Dellosa
Basics

Count and Move Cards

Cut out the pictures. Use them
with the Count and Move game.

Phoneme Hop

Get students hopping with excitement to count phonemes! Ahead of time, program a set of index cards with words and their corresponding number of phonemes (between three and five for each word). Suggested words and their numbers of phonemes are: *back (3)*, *ball (3)*, *fog (3)*, *desk (4)*, *bug (3)*, *fell (3)*, *sum (3)*, *net (3)*, *rock (3)*, *brick (4)*, *block (4)*, *lift (4)*, *fluff (4)*, *glass (4)*, *stop (4)*, *stamp (5)*, *rip (3)*, and *man (3)*. Program another set of index cards by writing a number three, four, or five on each card. Take students outside to an area with a clear starting line and finish line. (Cracks in the sidewalk, painted lines on a basketball court, and chalk lines on a playing field will all work.) Have students stand on the starting line, and give each student an index card with a number. Draw a card from the set of word/phoneme cards, say the word, and instruct students to count the number of sounds in the word. Call on one student to guess the number. If the number is correct, students should look at their index cards. A student whose card is programmed with a number that matches the number of phonemes in the word should take that many hops (or jumps) toward the finish line. For example, if the word is *gum*, a student with an index card that reads "3" should take three hops toward the finish line. Continue to say words until all students cross the finish line. The first few students who reach the finish line must wait for the others and continue to count the number of phonemes in the words.

I Spy!

Give each student a piece of white paper to fold in half twice to make four small pages. Have students unfold the papers and cut along the fold lines. (Very young students will need the pages supplied for them.) Help each student staple the pages together to make a mini-book. Tell students that they will make *I Spy* books and have students write the words *I Spy* on their book covers. Say, "I spy, with my little eye, a pen." Hold up a pen or a picture of one and ask, "How many sounds do you hear in the word *pen*?" Students should identify three separate sounds. Continue by saying, "Let's write the word *pen* in our *I Spy* books. Instruct students to turn to the first page. What's the first sound you hear in the word *pen*? The letter *p* makes the /p/ sound, so let's write the letter *p* on the page." Write the letter on the board. Continue in the same way with the remaining letters in the word *pen*. When you have sounded out and written the letters *e* and *n*, say, "We have just written the word *pen*. It has three sounds: /p/, short /e/, /n/." Touch each letter on the board as you say its sound. In his book, have each student draw a picture of a pen above the word. Find three more items for students to put in their *I Spy* books. Some suggestions for words include *cat*, *dog*, *hat*, *red*, *desk*, and student names that only have three or four sounds, like *Jim* and *Abby*.

syl·la·ble

Basic Syllabication

Introduction:

Syllabication is breaking words into word parts that are usually larger than phonemes and that contain a single vowel sound. Students should learn this skill after they have worked with breaking words into phonemes. Although syllabication is often not taught as part of phonemic awareness, it is an important phonemic and phonics skill that leads to vocabulary work and reading later on.

Feeling Syllables

Explain that words can be broken into small chunks of sound called *syllables*. These chunks are larger than phonemes. Students can hear and even feel syllables when pronouncing words. Direct students to place their elbows on a table, then have them place their chins in their hands. Tell students that when they say a word, their chins will press into their hands. Each time their chins press into their hands, it is a syllable. Students will be able to count syllables by counting the number of times their chins press into their hands. Have students say the word *boat* while their chins are in their hands. Ask, "How many times did your chins press into your hands when you said the word *boat*?" Students should feel one syllable. Say, "There is one syllable in the word *boat*." Tell students to say the word *flower* while they have their chins in their hands. Ask, "How many times did your chins press into your hands?" Confirm that there are two syllables in the word *flower*. Using the words *cheese (1)*, *page (1)*, *shadow (2)*, *bite (1)*, *weather (2)*, *museum (3)*, *stick (1)*, and *kindergarten (4)*, ask students to count the syllables using this method. If students are confused between breaking words into syllables and breaking them into phonemes, remind them that they are working with whole words, not individual sounds in words.

Applause, Please

Explain that syllables are small chunks of sound in a word. One way to count syllables is to clap while saying each syllable. Tell students to clap at natural pauses in a word. Help students remember by telling them that they should be impressed with a word that has more than one syllable, so they should clap more for words with more syllables. Bigger words deserve more applause. Say a few words that have various numbers of syllables and clap as you say each syllable. Allow students to practice this concept by clapping these words according to their numbers of syllables: *flat (1)*, *bike (1)*, *cage (1)*, *music (2)*, *birthday (2)*, *pencil (2)*, *strawberry (3)*, *September (3)*, and *beautiful (3)*. Have students give themselves a round of applause at the end for doing a great job counting syllables!

Drumming to the Beat

Gather students in a circle on the floor. Remind them that syllables are small chunks of sound in a word. Tell them that another good way to count syllables is to tap, or drum, them out. Have students be "syllable drummers." Give each student a craft stick or unsharpened pencil to tap out syllables on the floor. Explain that there is a rhythm to a word. Students can hear the syllables of the word when they say it. Demonstrate by saying the word *twinkle* and tapping the syllables on the floor. Ask students to count as you tap the syllables. Give students a chance to drum out the syllables as you say the word *twinkle*. Have them repeat the word after you. Then, instruct students to say, "twinkle" as they drum the syllables on the floor. Afterwards, ask, "How many syllables does the word *twinkle* have?" Students should answer that it has two syllables. Say the word *little*, and again, have students repeat the word and then drum out the syllables. Ask how many syllables *little* has. Repeat with the word *star*. Now, challenge students to tap out the syllables as they say the entire song title with you: "Twinkle, Twinkle, Little Star." Ask if anyone can count the syllables in the entire title. Continue in the same way with similar song titles, such as "Mary Had a Little Lamb," "The Farmer in the Dell," and "Happy Birthday to You."

Syllable Spin

Make one copy of the Syllable Spin reproducible (page 35). Use a paper fastener to attach a paper clip to the middle of the spinner. Test the spinner to make sure it moves smoothly before starting the lesson. Review various ways to count syllables; students can put their chins in their hands, clap, or tap on the floor or their desks. Play a game called Syllable Spin. Show the spinner and point out the numbers *1, 2,* and *3*. Have a volunteer spin the spinner. When the spinner stops on a number, direct each student to walk around the room and find something whose name has that number of syllables in it. For example, if the spinner lands on the number *1*, each student must find something in the room that has one syllable, such as a *pen, chair, book,* etc. If the spinner lands on the number *2*, each student must find something in the room that has two syllables, such as a *table, backpack, sweater,* etc. The big challenge will be if the spinner lands on the *3*! Students may find things such as a *library, calendar,* a classmate named *Jessica,* etc. After students search, call on volunteers to share their words. If students seem proficient at this activity, create another spinner with numbers 1–4. Throughout the day, add four-syllable words (*watercolors, radiator, California* on a map, *caterpillar* in a book title, etc.).

First-Rate Reading™: Phonemic Awareness and Phonics • CD-104018 • © Carson-Dellosa
Basics

Syllable Spin

Cut out the spinner. Use a paper
fastener to attach a large paper clip to the "X."

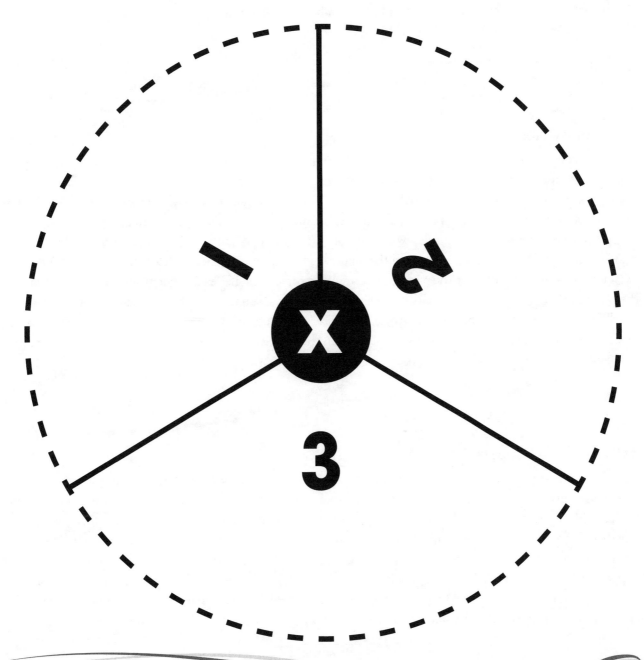

Syllable Song

Remind students of the different ways to count syllables (pages 33–34). Sing the following song to the tune of "London Bridge Is Falling Down." If desired, teach students the response. At the end of the first verse, call on a student to use one of the methods to count the syllables in his name. Repeat the "Syllable Song" until all students have the opportunity to count the syllables in their names.

"Syllable Song"
Count the syllables in your name,
In your name, in your name.
Count the syllables in your name,
My dear (student's name).

Student Response:
I have (number) syllables in my name,
In my name, in my name.
I have (number) syllables in my name,
My dear teacher.

Sacks of Syllables

Make one copy of the Sacks of Syllables reproducible (page 37) and cut apart the picture cards. Draw the number 1 on a large paper grocery bag, the number 2 on another grocery bag, and the number 3 on a third bag. Remind students of the different ways to count syllables (pages 33–34). Give each student a different picture card. Make sure each student can identify her picture. (Picture names are *flower, strawberry, apple, snake, calendar, toothbrush, newspaper, cookie, house, duck, umbrella, basketball, candy, moon, clock, car, pizza, volcano, feather,* and *key*.) Ask students to count the number of syllables in the names of their pictures. When students have counted their syllables, work with them to sort the picture cards into the three bags. Let each student show her picture card, say the name of the picture, then identify the number of syllables in the name. Ask the rest of the class if the number of syllables is correct. Share the correct answer, then direct the student to place the picture in the appropriate grocery bag. Repeat with the rest of the students. When the activity is complete, remove the cards and store them in a center with the bags so that students can have individual practice.

Syllable Sock Puppets

Ask each student to bring in a pair of clean, matching socks. Select enough pairs for each student to have just one sock, and return the remaining pairs. Distribute one sock to each student. Have each student place the sock on his hand like a sock puppet. Explain that the classmate with the matching sock is his partner. Have partners sit together. Say a two-syllable word and let partners work together to count and identify each syllable in the word. Then, one partner should have his sock puppet "say" the first syllable and the other partner should have her sock puppet "say" the second syllable. For example, if the word is *puppet*, the first student's sock puppet would say *pup* and the second sock puppet would say *pet*. Repeat with additional two-syllable words. For an added challenge, assign students to groups of three and repeat the activity with three-syllable words.

Sacks of Syllables

Cut apart the picture cards. Sort
the one-, two-, and three-syllable words.

Introduction

Phoneme manipulation involves three related skills: phoneme deletion, addition, and substitution. Phoneme deletion requires students to drop a phoneme from a word. For example, if students hear the word *fox*, they should be able to drop the /f/ to leave *ox*. Phoneme addition requires students to add a phoneme to a word to make a new word. For example, students should be able to add /s/ to *mile* to make *smile*. Finally, phoneme substitution requires students to exchange one phoneme for another. For example, students could change the /r/ in *rug* to a /b/ to make *bug*. Teach these concepts separately at first, then combine them as students become more skilled.

Deleting Phonemes

Remind students that words have individual sounds. For example, the word *bug* is made up of the sounds /b/, short /u/, /g/. Select three students to come to the front of the classroom. Have the first student say the /k/ sound in the word *kite*, the second student say the long /i/ sound, and the third student say the /t/ sound. Ask the rest of the class to blend the sounds together. Then, demonstrate removing the first sound of the word by having the first student turn around. Direct the second and third students to say their sounds (long /i/, /t/). Have the class blend these remaining sounds (*-ite*) and allow these students to return to their seats. Select three different students to come to the front of the classroom. This time, have students say the three sounds in the word *leaf* (/l/, long /e/, /f/). Ask the class to blend the sounds together to say the entire word. Then ask, "What would the word sound like if we didn't say the first sound?" Have the first student turn around while the remaining two students say their sounds (long /e/, /f/). Direct the rest of the class to blend the remaining sounds (*-eaf*). Repeat the process with different words. After students have practiced several times, continue to call on volunteers, but have individual students blend the sounds in the word after the first sound has been removed.

Drop the First Sound

Give each student a paper cutout of the letter *r*. Explain that sounds in words can be separated in different ways. For example, say the word *rock*, then say the first sound (/r/) and then the rest of the word (*-ock*) separately. Explain that the letters before the first vowel are called the *onset*, and the rest of the word is called the *rime*. Have students make two fists. Guide each student to say the first sound of the word *run* as he lifts his left fist. Next, have each student say the rest of the word as he lifts his right fist. Practice several times. Then, tell each student to hold the paper *r* in his left hand and say the beginning sound of the word *ride* as he holds up the letter *r*. Have him say the rest of the word (*-ide*). Ask, "What would the word sound like if we dropped the beginning /r/ sound?" Have the student drop the paper *r* onto his desk and identify the rest of the word. Other words to use with this activity could be *race*, *rag*, *rain*, *rake*, *rat*, *red*, *rip*, and *roof*. As students focus on new letters, repeat the activity with words that begin with those letters.

Erase the Sound

Give each student an eraser (any type). Remind students that words have individual sounds. Have students "erase" the beginning sounds of words. Say the word *cap*. Direct students to lift their erasers in the air and pretend to erase the beginning sound of the word *cap* (/k/). Ask, "How would you say the word if we erased the /k/ sound from *cap*?" Students should respond with *-ap*. Repeat for the word *five*. Students should respond with *-ive*. Continue the lesson with the words: *boat* (*-oat*), *dear* (*-ear*), *flake* (*-lake*), *ring* (*-ing*), *seal* (*-eal*), and *toast* (*-oast*).

Add a Sound

Give each student a sentence strip and a copy of the Add a Sound reproducible (page 40) on white construction paper. Explain that chefs add ingredients to bowls and mix them together. Have students be "sound chefs." First, have each student cut out the chef's hat on the reproducible and tape it to a sentence strip. Wrap a sentence strip around each student's head and tape the ends together to make a hat. Next, begin mixing the sounds. Place a real bowl and wooden spoon in front of you. Pretend to put the word *rush* in the bowl, then pretend to add a /b/ sound to the word *rush* in the bowl and "mix" the letters with the spoon. Say, "Let's see what word I get when I add a /b/ sound

to the word *rush*." Repeat the sounds /b/-*rush*, /b/-*rush*, until you blend the sounds to make *brush*. Next, have students pretend that they have bowls and spoons in front of them. Have students pretend to put the word *rip* in their bowls, then mix in the /g/ sound. Ask, "What word do we have if we add /g/ to *rip*?" Help students blend the sounds to make *grip*. To finish the activity, add /k/ to *rib* to make *crib*; add /s/ to *led* to make *sled*, add /p/ to *lay* to make *play*, and add /s/ to *nap* to make *snap*.

Meanut Mutter Day

Before beginning this activity, get parental permission and inquire about students' food allergies and religious or other food preferences. Give each student one spoonful of peanut butter. (A large marshmallow will also work.) When students eat the peanut butter, immediately ask them to try to talk. Explain that the peanut butter makes it hard to say words clearly. Have them all say the /m/ sound and ask if it is still easy to make this sound while eating peanut butter. (It should be.) After students finish their peanut butter and drink water, explain that their words sounded like they were stuck together, but they could manage to make the /m/ sound at the beginning of every word. Tell students that they will speak "Meanut Mutter" by taking off the beginning sounds of several words and substituting the /m/ sound. For example, the word *teacher* becomes *meacher*, and the word *pencil* becomes *mencil*. Let each student say her name "Meanut Mutter" style. Hold up various objects and have students substitute the beginning sounds with the /m/ sound.

Add a Sound

Cut out the hat. Tape the hat
to a sentence strip.

Mystery Match

Give each student a copy of the Phoneme Manipulation reproducible (page 42). Have students cut apart the picture cards. Explain that each picture card has a match. If students take off the first sound of one picture card and substitute it with another sound, they will find its match. For example, have students find the picture of the cat. Ask, "What would the word *cat* sound like without its first sound?" Say, "*-at*" with students, then ask, "What would the word sound like if we added a /b/ sound to the beginning of *-at*?" After students answer *bat*, ask, "Is there a picture of a bat? The mystery match for the picture of the cat is *bat*." Have students place the two pictures next to each other. Direct students to find the *cake* card. Ask students to take off the first sound and add the /r/ sound, then find the mystery match (*rake*). Direct students to place those two pictures together. The rest of the mystery matches are *five* and *hive*, *hose* and *nose*, *can* and *fan*, and *net* and *jet*.

Silly Substitutions

Give each student a copy of the Phoneme Manipulation reproducible (page 42). Have students cut apart the cards. Each day, choose a different consonant sound for students to use to make silly substitutions. Have students substitute different consonant sounds for the beginning sounds of the names of the pictures. (Picture names are listed in Mystery Match, above.) For example, if the consonant sound of the day is /k/, have students find the picture of the cake. Direct students to substitute the /m/ sound for the initial /k/ sound in the word *cake*. Tell students to pronounce the word *make*. Ask, "Is that a silly substitution?" Students should recognize that *make* is a real word. Do the same thing with the words *hive*, *can*, *net*, *bat*, and *nose*, and have a volunteer tell whether each word is a real word. Change the silly substitution letter sound each day. Before each lesson, make sure the substitutions that make words are appropriate for school.

Phoneme Manipulation

Cut out the picture cards. Listen to your teacher tell you how to use them.

Letter Recognition

Introduction

As students learn how sounds work together, they must begin to put symbols with those sounds. Those symbols are *graphemes*, or letters and letter combinations, that are responsible for "telling" readers what sounds to make within words. The following lessons encompass learning the alphabet and general letter-sound recognition, as well as teach students that they have to combine letters to get some common sounds.

Alphabet Books

Alphabet books are effective tools for teaching students letter recognition. Alphabet books show students the letter sequence, and they also build vocabulary and strengthen beginning oral language. When using an alphabet book, share the entire book first. When you are ready to work on specific letters, focus on them by asking students to find the letter in the alphabet book and having them trace the letter in the air. Consider having students make their own alphabet books based on the book they are reading. Teach only one or two letters a day; any more will confuse students. Some recommended alphabet books include *Animalia* by Graeme Base (Harry N. Abrams, 1993), *Chicka Chicka Boom Boom* by Bill Martin, Jr., and John Archambault (Scholastic, 1989), *Eating the Alphabet: Fruits and Vegetables from A to Z* by Lois Ehlert (Harcourt, 1993), *On Market Street* by Arnold Lobel (HarperTrophy, 1989), and *The Z Was Zapped* by Chris Van Allsburg (Houghton Mifflin, 1987).

Find the Letter

Ahead of time, choose one consonant to introduce to students. On construction paper, trace and cut out enough copies of the consonant for each student to have one. Give each student a letter and a ruler, straw, or large craft stick. Explain that letters represent the sounds in words. If students know what each letter looks like and what sound it makes, they will be able to read. Write the letter of the day on the board. Introduce the letter to students by saying its name and describing how to write it. Have students trace the paper letters with their fingers. Then, tell each student to tape the letter to the end of his ruler. Direct each student to walk around the classroom with his letter and try to find another one somewhere in the room. Students may use classroom posters, books, bulletin boards, etc., to find matches for their letters. Have students share their matches. Read the words that begin with the letter of the day. Repeat the lesson with different letters on different days.

Letter Portraits

Students enjoy working with their own names. Introduce a new letter to the class by using students' names. Choose a letter of the day and write it on the board. Show students how to write the letter. Ask all students who have names that begin with that letter to stand in front of the board. For example, if the letter is s, students named Simon, Samantha, and Sherika should stand in front of the board. Write each student's name on the board above the student as you read the name aloud. Point out the first letter (not sound) in each student's name. Give each student a piece of drawing paper with writing lines at the bottom. Direct each student to choose one of her classmates who is standing at the front of the classroom and write the student's name on the lines. Remind the class how to write the letter of the day, then have each student draw a picture of the classmate above the writing. (Students at the front of the class may also complete the exercise.) Change letters each week so that different students stand in front of the classroom. When you have used all of the beginning letters of students' names, have students create pages for the missing letters by drawing and naming imaginary people. Have each student assemble the pages into a book, and add a cover and the title *My Letter Friends*.

Use Your Feet

Use this kinesthetic activity to teach letter recognition. Select a letter to introduce to students. Show them how to write the letter on the board. Say the name of the letter as a class, then let students write the letter. Take the class outside to a place where they can safely write on concrete or asphalt. Give each student a piece of chalk. Draw several copies of the letter on the concrete. Have students trace the letter with their feet. Then, have students draw the same letter on the concrete and trace the letter with their feet. Back in the classroom, give each student a piece of dark-colored construction paper. Using chalk, have students practice writing the letter on the paper. Throughout the day, have students "think on their feet" by tracing the letter on the floor with their feet.

Soft, Scratchy, Squishy Letters

Applying a multisensory approach can help different types of learners. In this lesson, students use the sense of touch to learn their letters. Choose a letter for students to learn. Explain that letters make up words and that when students learn their letters and sounds, they will be ready to read. Write the letter of the day on the board as you explain how to write it. Give each student a piece of construction paper, several cotton balls, and glue. Have students write the letter on the papers. Check to make sure each student has written the letter correctly. Then, direct students to glue the cotton balls onto the letters. When the glue is dry, encourage students to touch the cotton, tracing over it with their fingers as if they are writing it. Consider having students make textured letters with sand and take students to the sandbox. Or, let students squirt shaving cream letter shapes on their desks, then wipe the desks clean with damp paper towels.

Pair of Letters

Copy the Pair of Letters reproducibles (pages 46–48) and the cards below. Cut apart the cards. Give each student a matching uppercase and lowercase letter pair. Explain that each letter has an uppercase and lowercase version—they come in pairs, like shoes. Have each student study her cards, then tape the uppercase letter to her left shoe and the lowercase letter to her right shoe. Take one shoe from each student. Place the shoes in different piles around the classroom. Tell the class that when you say "Letter Pair," each student should try to find her matching letter and shoe in the piles, and put on the shoe when she finds it. Let students wear the letters for the remainder of the day.

Mary Had an Alphabet

Before this activity, trace and cut out the letters *a*, *b*, and *c*. Hide the letters around the room. Sing the song "Mary Had a Little Lamb" with students. Tell students that in a new version, Mary had an alphabet. Sing the following song to the same tune.

Mary had an alphabet,
al-pha-bet, al-pha-bet.
Mary had an alphabet whose letters looked like these . . .
(Write the letters *a*, *b*, and *c* on the board.)

They followed her to school one day,
school one day, school one day.
They followed her to school one day
And hid so carefully.

Then, ask students if they can find the letters *a*, *b*, and *c* in the classroom. Let the three students who find the letters sing the song, then hide the letters again when students are out of the classroom. Repeat so that several students have a chance to find the letters. To vary the activity, do not hide letters, but suggest that students look at posters, books, and bulletin boards to find them. Have students share their discoveries. Vary the letters from week to week. When students recognize all letters, hide all of them, but ask students to find three at a time.

Pair of Letters

Cut apart the cards. Use
with the activity "Pair of Letters."

A	**a**	**B**	**b**
C	**c**	**D**	**d**
E	**e**	**F**	**f**
G	**g**	**H**	**h**

First-Rate Reading™: Phonemic Awareness and Phonics • CD-104018 • © Carson-Dellosa
Basics

Pair of Letters

Cut apart the cards. Use
with the activity "Pair of Letters."

I	i	J	j
K	k	L	l
M	m	N	n
O	o	P	p

Pair of Letters

Cut apart the cards. Use
with the activity "Pair of Letters."

Q	**q**	**R**	**r**
S	**s**	**T**	**t**
U	**u**	**V**	**v**
W	**w**	**X**	**x**

First-Rate Reading™: Phonemic Awareness and Phonics • CD-104018 • © Carson-Dellosa
Basics

Letter Bingo

Draw a Tic-Tac-Toe grid on a piece of paper. Copy the grid for each student, and give each student nine counters, pennies, or other manipulatives to mark spaces. Select nine letters that students have studied and write them on the board. Also write the letters on small pieces of paper (or use the Pair of Letters cards on pages 45–48) and place them in a bag or hat. Review the letter names and have each student copy the letters on her grid in random order using each letter only once. Next, play Letter Tic-Tac-Toe. Pull a letter out of the bag and say its name. Tell students to look on their grids for the letter. When they find it, have students place a counter on the letter. Direct students to say, "Tic-Tac-Toe!" when they get three counters in a horizontal, vertical, or diagonal row. Continue to call out letters until several students get three counters in a row. Have students swap cards and start the game over.

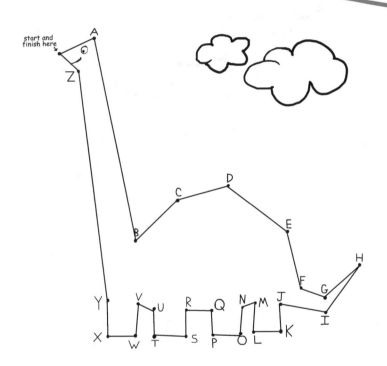

Connect the Letters

Ahead of time, copy the Connect the Letters reproducible (page 50) for each student. Explain that there is a letter beside each dot. Have students connect the dots in alphabetical order to reveal the picture. Then, help each student write his first name at the top of his picture. Post the dot-to-dot pictures in alphabetical order by students' first names. Completed pictures should look like the dinosaur picture to the left.

Which Letter?

Review letter recognition by playing Which Letter? Post an alphabet chart in the room for students to reference. Choose a letter but do not reveal it. Give visual clues about the letter, such as, "This letter is made up of four straight lines. It is an uppercase letter, but the lowercase letter looks the same, except it is smaller. It looks a little like two of the letter V joined together." Continue giving clues until a student recognizes that the letter being described is a W. Repeat with other letters. Remember to differentiate between uppercase and lowercase letters early when giving clues.

Connect the Letters

Follow the alphabet
to connect the dots.

start and
finish here

A

O

Z

D

C

E

B

H

F

Y   V   U   R   Q   N   M   J   G

I

X   W   T   S   P   O   L   K

First-Rate Reading™: Phonemic Awareness and Phonics • CD-104018 • © Carson-Dellosa
Basics

Consonant Sounds

give me a "T"-"t"

Introduction

Most schools and districts insist that teachers use particular phonics programs that teach letters in a systematic and sequential order. These activities teach students to link sounds to specific consonants and can be taught in any order. Choose activities based on your phonics program or in any order you wish as a review.

Bounce the Balloon

To prepare, blow up a balloon or beach ball. Explain that words are made of letters, and each letter has a sound. Tell students that learning letter sounds will help them read. Start this activity with the letter *b*. Write *b* on the board. Explain that *b* makes a /b/ sound as in the word *balloon* (or *beach ball*). Show the balloon and say, "You can also hear the /b/ sound at the beginning of the word *bounce*." Write the word *bounce* on the board. Toss the balloon to a student. When the student catches the balloon, have her say another word that starts with the letter *b*. Add her word to the list on the board. Have the student toss the balloon back to you. Toss the balloon to another student and ask him to say a *b* word. Repeat until each student has had a turn, then read the word list and have students repeat. (Before completing any balloon activity, check for possible latex allergies, and note that popped or uninflated balloons may present a choking hazard.)

Letter Mobiles

Remind students that each letter has a name, shape, and sound. Ask students to identify the first letters in their names and tell if they are consonants. Ask, "What sound does that letter make?" On separate pieces of paper, let students practice writing the first letters of their names. Then, copy one Letter Fun reproducible (page 53) for every four students. Have students cut out the cards. Give each student three of the cards, a wire coat hanger, three pieces of yarn, and tape. Let students identify the picture names on the cards. (See Guess the Letter on page 52 for picture names.) Tell each student to think about the sound at the beginning of each picture's name. Direct students to write the first letter of the picture's name on the back of the picture. Have each student tape one end of a piece of yarn to the picture and tape or tie the other end to the wire hanger. Hang the letter mobiles around the classroom.

Letter Sounds in Literature

Use children's literature to teach letter sounds in context. For example, to teach /f/, read *The Foot Book* by Dr. Seuss (Random House, 1968). After a first reading, reread the book, but this time point out the words that start with the /f/ sound. As you reread, have students stomp their feet each time they hear the /f/ sound. Ask students to brainstorm other words that start with the same sound. Use the same activity with a different book to teach other letters. The story *What Pete Ate from A–Z* (M. Kalman, Puffin Books, 2001) weaves several words together that all start with the same sound. Read the entire book aloud, then choose one or two letters to work on. Think of unusual ways to ask students to identify words that begin with that sound. For example, have them hiss like snakes each time they hear an /s/ sound, or they can make s-shapes with their hands and raise them when they see the letter.

Consonant Cheer

Get "fired up" to learn letter sounds with this alphabet cheer. Write a letter on a large piece of paper. Say the cheer below to the same rhythm as, "Two, four, six, eight, who do we appreciate? The Bears! The Bears! Ya-a-ay, Bears!" Say the cheer to the class: "A, B, C, D! Give that letter sound to me! Letters! Letters. Ya-a-ay, letters!" Then, as you show the letter card, say, "Give me a sound! Give me a sound! What's that sound?" After each sentence, hold up the letter card. When you say, "Give me a sound!" have students say the sound of the letter back to you. For example, if you hold up a card with a *t* on it and say "Give me a sound!" students should say the /t/ sound. Repeat the cheer as many times as desired.

Guess the Letter

Pair students. Give each pair a copy of the Letter Fun reproducible (page 53). Review the picture names and identify the beginning letter of each picture's name. (Picture names are *car, duck, wagon, bear, gum, mouse, heart, lion, pig, sock, tape,* and *fan.*) Say the picture name *bear* and ask, "What letter makes the /b/ sound?" Direct each student to write the beginning letter *b* on or next to the picture. Repeat with the remaining cards. Have students cut apart the picture cards and play a game. Have pairs place their sets of cards facedown on the floor, mix up the cards, then restack them. Tell Player A to pick a card and say the word to the other player. Instruct Player B to listen to the beginning sound of the word and try to identify the beginning letter. Player A should look at the letter written on the card, tell Player B if he is correct, and show Player B the answer. If Player B is correct, he may keep the card. Have the players alternate turns. The player with the most cards at the end of the game wins.

Small Wall

Help students make personal word walls as you introduce consonants. Give each student a copy of both Small Wall reproducibles (pages 54–55), several index cards, and a manila folder. Explain that all consonants in the alphabet are on these two pages. (Define *consonants* if students are not familiar with the word.) Remind students that each letter has its own sound. Write the letter *s* on the board. Tell students that the *s* sounds like /s/ as in *snake.* Write the word *snake* and draw a simple snake on the board. Direct students' attention to their small word walls. Have each student write *-nake* on the line by the letter *s.* Then, let each student draw a snake on an index card, cut out the letter card, and staple the letter card to the index card. Write each letter on the board and explain the sound. When you come to the letter *x,* tell students that very few words begin with *x,* but several words end with *x,* such as *box, fox, six,* etc. Have students write and draw words that end with *x.* Repeat with one or two different letters each week to teach the sound of each consonant, and have students store their cards and letters in the folders. Or, give each student a piece of poster board on which to glue the index cards. Encourage students to use their small word walls when they cannot remember letters and their sounds, and also during writing activities.

Letter Fun

Cut out the picture cards. Listen to your teacher tell you how to use them.

Small Wall

Write a word for each consonant.
Draw a matching picture on an index card.
Attach each word to the top, left corner of the matching index card.

b _____

c _____

d _____

f _____

g _____

h _____

j _____

k _____

l _____

m _____

First-Rate Reading™: Phonemic Awareness and Phonics Basics • CD-104018 • © Carson-Dellosa

Small Wall

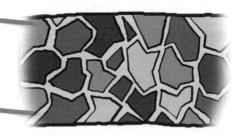

Write a word for each consonant.
Draw a matching picture on an index card.
Attach each word to the top, left corner of the matching index card.

n _____

p _____

q _____

r _____

z

s _____

t _____

v _____

w _____

_____ x

y _____

Sound Menu

Give a copy of your school's cafeteria menu and a paper plate to each student. (School lunch menus are often available on-line.) Choose a letter sound that is repeated on the menu. Write the letter on the board. Tell the class the sound that the letter makes and have them repeat it back to you. Give students a sample word that begins with that letter. Write it on the board and move your finger under the word as you pronounce it. Direct students to find and circle words on their menus that start with the chosen letter. After most students have finished, call on each student to spell one of her words. Write each student's word on the board and read it aloud. After getting several responses, have each student write one of the words from the board on her paper plate. Cover a bulletin board with strips of red and white bulletin board paper to make a checkerboard pattern like a tablecloth. Staple the plates to the bulletin board. Title the board "Letters from Lunch."

School Lunch
for the week of March 12th–16th

Monday: Cheese or pepperoni pizza, tossed salad with dressing, raisins

Tuesday: Spicy tacos with cheese, corn, chips and salsa, lettuce and tomatoes, pears

Wednesday: Chicken or veggie nuggets, corn on the cob, broccoli and cheese, spiced apples

Thursday: Veggie burgers, baked beans, tater tots, carrot sticks, grapes

Friday: Turkey or veggie wraps, cucumber slices, bananas, fruit cups

Dictation

Take an informal assessment of students' letter/sound knowledge by dictating sounds. Give each student a piece of paper and a pencil. Say a sound, then say a word that begins with that sound. Finally, repeat the sound again. Instruct students to write the letter that makes that sound. For example, if you say "/r/, rock, /r/," students should write the letter *r*. Choose only five or six consonants for the dictation. To get a bigger picture of students' progress, repeat this activity each day with five or six different consonants. Do not give students letters that sound similar (such as /b/ and /d/) unless you say another letter in between.

Short Vowel Sounds

trăsh căn

Introduction

Different phonics programs teach vowel sounds in different orders. Some programs teach long vowel sounds first because the letters "say their names." Other programs assume that letter and sound knowledge is more easily acquired by teaching short vowels first because short vowel sounds require no "tricks" (silent e, vowel teams, etc.) to make the sounds. Follow your phonics program when deciding how to structure vowel sound instruction.

Thinking Caps

Copy the Building with Short Vowels reproducible (page 58) for each student. Also, give each student a piece of bulletin board paper. Explain that five letters of the alphabet are called *vowels*. (Instruct students about the letter *y* according to your phonics program.) Vowels are used to build words, and each vowel has its own sounds. Have each student cut apart the letter cards, then place the letters *c*, *a*, *p*, *t*, and *n* in front of her. Give each student a resealable, plastic bag to store her remaining letters for other activities. Tell students that the letter *a* is a vowel. Short /a/ sounds like the middle of the word *hat*. Write *hat* on the board, say the sounds of each letter, and blend them into the whole word. Direct students to find the letters *c*, *a*, and *p*, and place them on their desks to spell the word *cap*. Ask, "What sound does the letter *c* make?" Remind students of the short /a/ sound. Then ask, "What sound does the letter *p* make?" After students answer, say, "Let's blend all three sounds together: /k/-/a/-/p/. Does that sound like a word to you? What word is /k/-/a/-/p/?" Write *cap* on the board. Repeat the process with other short /a/ words such as *can*, *pan*, *nap*, *tap*, and *cat*. Write each word on the board as you teach it. Direct each student to choose one of the short /a/ words from the board to write on his piece of bulletin board paper. Then, have each student tape together the ends of his paper around his head to make a hat. Have students wear their hats and try to read the words on other students' hats.

Big Pigs

Give each student one copy each of the Building with Short Vowels reproducible (page 58) and the Big Pigs reproducible (page 59). Explain that the letter *i* is a vowel used with other letters to build words. Tell students that short /i/ is in the middle of the word *dig*. Write *dig* on the board and say the sound of each letter as you track the print. Blend the sounds together to make the word *dig*. Direct each student to cut apart the letters and place the *p*, *i*, and *g* in front of him. Ask, "What sound does the letter *p* make?" Remind students about the sound of short /i/. Then ask, "What sound does the letter *g* make?" Guide students as they blend the sounds. Have students identify the word *pig*. Write the word *pig* on the board. Continue by having students make the words *big*, *tip*, *pit*, and *bit*, and write them on the board. Have each student choose one of the short /i/ words from the board and write it on the pig on the Big Pigs reproducible. Ask each student to cut out his pig. Post the pigs on a bulletin board titled "We're Hog-Wild for Short /i/!"

Building with Short Vowels

Cut apart the letters. Listen
to your teacher tell you how to use them to make words.

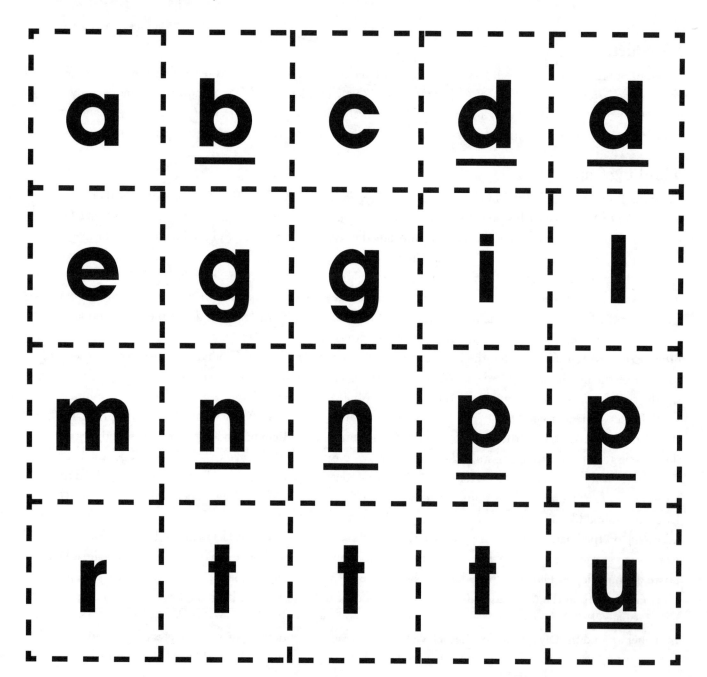

Big Pigs

Write a word on the pig
that uses the short /i/ sound. Cut out the pig.

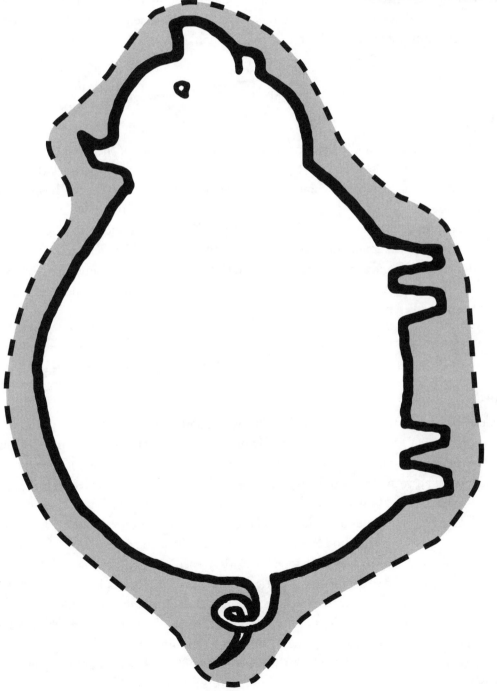

Soaking Up Sounds

Provide a mop for this activity. Give each student a paintbrush and a small bowl of water. Explain that the letter *o* is a vowel and is used to build words. Tell students that the letter *o* makes the short /o/ sound in the word *mop*. Write the word *mop* on the board and say it as you track the print. Have students take the paintbrushes and bowls of water outside to a concrete area. Explain that the brushes are like small *mops*. Have students dip their "mops" in the water then use them as you use the mop to write other short /o/ words, such as *top, not, pot, hop,* and *got*. First, direct students to "mop" the letters *t, o,* and *p*. Ask, "What sound does the letter *t* make?" Remind students of the short /o/ sound, then ask, "What sound does the letter *p* make?" Guide students in blending the sounds to make the word *top*. Have students call out other short /o/ words to "mop."

"Red-ing Words"

Explain that the letter *e* is a vowel and is used to build words. Tell students that the short /e/ sound is the sound in the middle of the word *red*. Write *red* on the board and say each letter sound as you track the print. Give each student a copy of the Building with Short Vowels reproducible (page 58) and a piece of red paper about the size of an index card. Have students cut apart the letter cards on the reproducible. (Or, have students use the letters *t, e, n, l,* and *d* from their resealable bags. See Thinking Caps, page 57.) Direct students to place the letters *t, e,* and *n* in front of them and to say the sounds until they blend into the word *ten*. Write *ten* on the board. Repeat with the short /e/ words *net, let, led,* and *den*, then have each student choose one of the short /e/ words to write on his red piece of paper. Allow students to read their words to each other. Staple the red words to a bulletin board titled "Red Alert! We Know the Letter E!"

Tug of Words

Give each student two index cards, a copy of the Building with Short Vowels reproducible (page 58), and a piece of string that is approximately 1' (about 30.5 cm) long. Explain that the letter *u* is a vowel used to build words. Tell students that short /u/ is in the middle of the word *tug*. Write *tug* on the board and say each letter as you track the print. Have students cut apart the cards on the reproducible, or have students use the letters *r, u, g, d, m,* and *b* from their resealable bags. (See Thinking Caps, page 57.) Direct students to place the letters *r, u,* and *g* in front of them. Guide students to say the sounds until they blend into the word *rug*. Write *rug* on the board. Repeat with other short /u/ words, such as *dug, mud,* and *bug*. Next, have each student choose two words from the board to write on her index cards. Direct each student to tape her cards to each end of the string, as if they are having a "tug of war." Staple the cards and string them in a vertical row on a bulletin board, leaving enough space on either side of the cards to write. Assign students to two teams and have the teams stand on opposite sides of the bulletin board. Ask the first team to name a short /u/ word that is not on the board. Write that team's suggestion on the appropriate side of the board and then let the other team have a turn. Repeat until students cannot think of more words. The team with the most short /u/ words on their side of the bulletin board wins the tug of war. Title the board "Tug of Words."

First-Rate Reading™: Phonemic Awareness and Phonics • CD-104018 • © Carson-Dellosa
Basics

"A" Frame

Give each student a chenille craft stick and a copy of the "A" Frame reproducible (page 62). Work with each student to bend the chenille craft stick to make a lowercase *a* by making a circle with the chenille craft stick, leaving a little extra at one end to make the tail of the *a*. Direct students to twist the chenille craft sticks to connect the ends. Ask, "What sound does short /a/ make?" Ask students to give examples of words with the short /a/ sound, such as *hat, cat, mat*, etc. Then, explain that each word on the reproducible has a vowel in it. Pair students with different reading levels and have pairs use their chenille-craft-stick letters to frame the words and then decode them. Call on several different students to read the short /a/ words.

Hop and Ten

Ask, "What sound does short /o/ make?" Tell students that the short /o/ sound makes the sound in the middle of the word *hop*. Write *hop* on the board, then ask, "What sound does short /e/ make?" Remind students that short /e/ sounds like the middle of the word *ten*. Write *ten* on the board. Explain that you will say a word that has either a short /o/ sound or a short /e/ sound in it. Tell students that if you say a word that has a short /o/ sound, they should *hop* (because *hop* has the short /o/ sound). When students hear a word with a short /e/ sound, they should hold up 10 fingers (because *ten* has the short /e/ sound). Use the words *bed, pet, fox, pot, leg, fox, fed*, and *fog* to complete the activity. To make this activity less challenging, have students focus on one sound.

Short /u/ Story

Write the letters *ug* on the board. Ask, "What sound does short /u/ make? What would the letters *t, u*, and *g* sound like?" Erase the letter *t* and let students try other consonants at the beginning of the *-ug* word family to make words, such as *mug, jug, rug, hug*, etc. Write the words on the board. Repeat with other short /u/ word families, such as *-un, -ub*, and *-up*. Challenge each student to make a sentence with as many short /u/ words as he can. Encourage students to use the words on the board and other words they know. Give an example, such as, "The bug on the bus went for fun in the sun." Call on students to say sentences, then have each student write and illustrate a sentence using as many short /u/ words as he can. Collect the sentences into a class book titled *Short /u/ Stories by Us*.

"A" Frame

Find the short /a/ words.
Frame them with your letter a. Read them.

bag

pet

box

hot   fun   sad

ran   lip   bug

had   dot

tip   rip

hen   map

First-Rate Reading™: Phonemic Awareness and Phonics • CD-104018 • © Carson-Dellosa
Basics

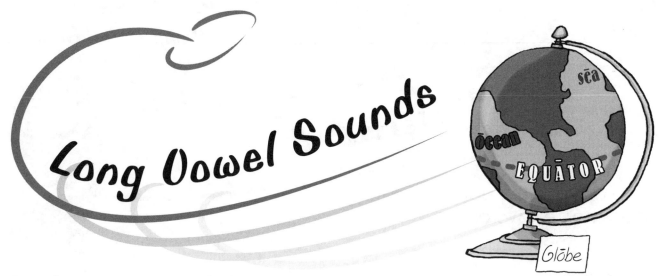

Long Vowel Sounds

Introduction

Students will enjoy learning to read words in which the vowels "say their names." These sounds should be familiar to students.

Make a Mental Note

Before beginning this activity, write the letter *e* on several sticky notes. Write the short vowel words *not, hop, rob,* and *rod* on a piece of chart paper. Post the chart paper and work with students to decode each word. Then, tell students that vowels have different sounds. If there is an *e* on the end of a word, it usually means the vowel will say its name and is called a *long vowel*. Take a sticky note with an *e* on it and place it at the end of the word *not*. Explain that the *e* on the end of the word is telling the vowel to say its name and make the long /o/ sound. Say each letter sound as you track print under the word *note*. Repeat that the *e* at the end of the word causes the vowel sound to change. Tell students that you will use other *e* notes to change the sounds of other words. Have students read each short vowel word. Place a sticky note with an *e* on the end of the word. Work with the class to read the new word. Repeat with the rest of the words to make *hope, robe,* and *rode.*

High-Flying Vowels

Give each student a kite-shaped piece of paper and a 1'-long (30.5 cm) piece of crepe paper or ribbon. Explain that the vowel sound in a word changes when there is an *e* on the end. Write the word *kit* on the board for students to read. Then, add *e* to the end and explain that the vowel now says its name. Read the word *kite* for students and track the print. Next, write the long /i/ words *five, hive, like, nice, nine,* and *side* on the board. Help students decode each word. Have students write the words on the kite-shaped papers, then tape the crepe paper strips or ribbons to the bottoms of the kites to make tails. Display the kites on a bulletin board titled "High-Flying Vowels."

Super E

Send a note home to ask permission for each student to bring in a bath towel, or let students make capes from bulletin board paper. Give each student a copy of the Super E reproducible (page 64). Explain that some words are made up of a consonant, a vowel, and a consonant (CVC). Write *cap* on the board and point out the consonant, vowel, and consonant. Tell students that when letters in words are CVC, the vowel is a short sound. Track the print as you pronounce the word *cap.* Next, tell students that if an *e* is added to the end of a CVC word, the vowel in the middle says its name. Write an *e* at the end of the word *cap.* Explain that the *e* at the end of the word makes the letter *a* say the long /a/ sound (its name). Read the new word *cape* aloud. Then, have students be superheroes by changing other words. Have each student hold the ends of her towel around her shoulders to make a cape. (If students use paper, write the letter *e* on each piece and tape it to the back of each student's shirt.) Tell each student that she has become the superhero known as "Super E." "Super E" can change words with one letter. Have students write an *e* at the end of each word on the reproducible. Then, call on the superheroes to decode the new CVCe words.

Super E

Write an "e" after each word.
Read the new words.

1. can__

2. cap__

3. dim__

4. fad__

5. fin__

6. hop__

7. mad__

8. man__

9. mop__

10. not__

11. pal__

12. pan__

13. pin__

14. tap__

First-Rate Reading™: Phonemic Awareness and Phonics • CD-104018 • © Carson-Dellosa
Basics

Go Team!

Use this activity to introduce vowel teams. Give each student a construction paper triangle shaped like a team pennant and a copy of the Building with Long Vowels reproducible (page 66). (Have each student save the letters in resealable, plastic bags labeled *long vowel letters* and use them in other activities.) Explain that separately, the letters *e* and *a* are short vowels, but together they are a long vowel team. When students see *ea* in a word, the sound they make is long /e/. Most of the time, when two vowels appear together, the first says its name, and the second is silent. Write the word *team* on the board. Say each sound as you track the print. Have each student cut out the following letters on the reproducible: *e, a, t, m, s, n,* and *l*. Have each student place the *ea* together in front of him. Then, model adding and taking away letters to make the following long /e/ words: *tea, eat, seat, meat, neat, meal, seal, mean,* and *lean*. Each time students make a word, have them try to read it. Encourage them to track the print as they blend the sounds. Write the *ea* words on the board. Tell students that because the letters *ea* are a vowel team, they will make team pennants. Have students turn their pennants so that they are pointing to the right, then let them write several *ea* words on them. Allow students to use the words from the board or think of their own. Display the pennants on a bulletin board titled "Go Vowel Team!"

Sailing Through

Continue work with vowel teams with this smooth-sailing activity. Ahead of time, cut a large piece of white bulletin board paper into the shape of a sail. Attach a brown, paper semicircle for the hull of the boat and black paper for a mast to create a sailboat. Explain that when two vowels are together in a word, the first vowel usually says its name while the second vowel is silent. For example, when the letters *oa* are together, the sound is long /o/ as in *boat*. Write the word *boat* on the board. Draw a line under the letters *oa* to show how the sounds blend together to form the word *boat*. Have each student cut out the following letter cards from the Building with Long Vowels reproducible (page 66): *o, a, g, d, l, c, t,* and *r*. Start with the letters *o, a,* and *t*. Work with students to form the words *goat* and *coat*. Suggest that students track the print as they blend the sounds together. Write the words on the board. Then, have the class find the letters *o, a,* and *l*. Direct students to make the words *goal* and *coal*. Add them to the list of words on the board. Repeat with the letters *o, a,* and *d* to make the words *load, toad,* and *road*. Ask, "What sound do the letters *oa* make together?" Place the large, white triangle on the floor. Tell students that the paper is the sail for the *oa* boat. Gather students on the floor and allow them to write *oa* words from the board or new words that they make with their letter cards on the sail. Write *oa boat* on the front to name the boat and staple the mast, sail, and boat together on a bulletin board. Title the bulletin board "Sailing on the Vowel Team Boat."

Building with Long Vowels

Cut apart the letters. Listen to
your teacher tell you how to use them to make words.

a	a	b	c	d	e
e	e	f	g	h	i
l	m	n	o	o	o
r	s	t	u	w	

First-Rate Reading™: Phonemic Awareness and Phonics • CD-104018 • © Carson-Dellosa
Basics

Mail Call

Explain that when two vowels are together in a word, they make one sound: the first vowel says its name and the second vowel is silent. Or, teach the mnemonic device, "When two vowels go walking, the first one does the talking." For example, when the letters *ai* are next to each other in a word, *a* says long /a/ and *i* is silent. Write the word *mail* on the board and draw a line under the letters *ai*. Show students how to decode the word by tracking the print and blending the sounds together.

Have students make other *ai* words. Have each student cut out the envelope and the strip of paper on the Mail Call reproducible (page 68), place his envelope horizontally in front of him, then fold it so that the slits are folded in half. Next, have him make a small cut along each folded slit line to the end and then open up the paper. Direct each student to weave the strip of paper through the slits so that the letters on the strip are visible through the slits as she pulls it through. Have students pull the strips so that they can see the first letter (*f*). Work with students to blend the sound of the first letter with the letters *a*, *i*, and *l*. Ask, "How would you read this word?" Tell students to pull the strip to show the *h*. Guide students to blend the sounds together to make the word *hail*. Write *hail* on the board. Repeat with the rest of the letters, then review the words on the board with the class. Underline the *ai* as you say each word. At the end of the lesson, ask, "What sound do the letters *ai* make when they are next to each other in a word?"

Flip It!

Review the different ways students have learned to make long vowel sounds (adding a silent e and vowel teams). Teach another way to make a long vowel sound. Explain that when a word has one syllable and ends in a vowel, the vowel sound is usually long. (Exceptions are *ha, ma, do,* etc.) For example, write the word *hi* on the board. Ask, "How many syllables does the word *hi* have? Does the word end in a vowel? Then, we know the vowel says its name. How would you pronounce this word?" Continue giving examples, such as *be, by, go, me, no, so, we,* etc., then play Flip It! Pair students. Give each pair a copy of the Building with Long Vowels reproducible (page 66). Have students cut out the letters *b, m, w, g, n, s,* three *e's,* and three *o's.* Tell students to place the consonants facedown on the left and place the vowels facedown on the right. Have Player A turn over one consonant and one vowel and then blend the sounds, keeping in mind that the vowel will have a long vowel sound. If the two letters make a word, Player A should keep the cards and it is Player B's turn. If the two letters do not make a word, Player A should turn the cards facedown and mix up each pile, and Player B should take a turn. Have players continue until there are no cards left. The player with the most cards at the end of the game is the winner.

Mail Call

Cut out the strip of letters. Cut out the envelope, and then cut the slits. Slide the strip of paper through the slits to make words.

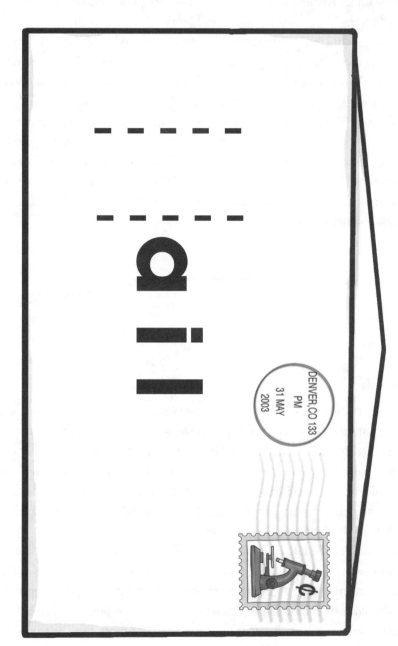

f h m n p r s t

a i l

DENVER, CO 133
PM
31 MAY
2003

Consonant Blends

Introduction

Understanding blends and digraphs enables students to read many of the words they will encounter in grade-appropriate reading. As you teach these concepts, supplement instruction with more reading materials.

Crabby Blends

Tell students that sometimes words have two consonants together called *blends* or *clusters*. Explain that when students say a blend, they say both consonant sounds. Write the word *crab* on the board. Underline the *cr* part of the word and say that it is a consonant blend. Pronounce the word *crab* as you track the print. Have students make more words with the consonant blend *cr*. Give each student a copy of the Consonant Blends reproducible (page 70). Have students cut apart the letter cards and save them in resealable, plastic bags for additional activities. Instruct students to find the letters *c, r, o,* and *p,* and place the letters in front of them. Challenge students to read the word *crop* as you write it on the board. Guide students to make the following words with their letter cards: *craft, crib, creek, creep, crust,* and *cry.* Write each word on the board after students decode the letters. Next, give each student a piece of white construction paper on which to draw a crab, then give the following directions:

1. Draw a large circle in the middle of the paper.
2. Draw two smaller circles above the large circle.
3. Draw a line from each small circle to the large circle below it.
4. Add dots inside the small circles for eyes.
5. Add eight lines along the bottom of the large circle for legs.
6. Draw two claws on either side of the large circle.

Direct students to write *cr* words on their crabs, then color them. On a sheet of bulletin board paper, have students draw a beach scene. Glue on real seashells if possible. Cover a table with the paper and place the crabs on top. Allow students to play with the crabs as they familiarize themselves with the *cr* words.

On Track

Train students to recognize the *tr* blend. Cut off the frog and octagon sections from the Blend Buddies reproducible (page 72), and copy the train engine for each student. Explain that some words have two consonants next to each other called consonant *blends*. Explain that when students see a blend, they should pronounce each letter's sound. Write *train* on the board. Underline the *tr*, identify it as a consonant blend, and tell students to listen for both letters when saying the word. Pronounce *train* for students to repeat. Guide students to use their letter cards to make *track, tree, true, trade, trap, trip,* and *trail.* Have each student use letters from the Consonant Blends reproducible (page 70). Next, distribute several index cards and a piece of yarn to each student. (The length of the yarn will depend on the number of cards—the more cards, the longer the yarn.) Tell each student to cut out the train engine, write at least three *tr* words on the index cards, and connect the engine and cards by gluing them to the yarn. Tape the trains end to end around the room. Add the title "We're on Track with Blends!" Or, tie a yarn loop to the top of every other card and string the trains across the room on a fishing line "track." Let students move the trains back and forth on the fishing line.

Consonant Blends

Cut apart the cards. Use them
to build words with consonant blends.

a	b	c	d	e	e
f	g	h	i	k	l
l	m	n	o	p	r
s	t	u	w	y	z

Froggy Friends

Continue to work on blends. Write the word *frog* on the board. Draw a line under the *fr* in the word *frog*. Tell students that the *fr* is a consonant blend. Say the word *frog* for students as you track the print. Give each student a copy of the frog section from the Blend Buddies reproducible (page 72) and a craft stick. Have students use the letters from the Consonant Blends reproducible (page 70). Direct students to color and cut out the frogs and glue them to the tops of the craft sticks to make frog puppets. Instruct students to find the letter cards *f, r, e,* and *e* and place the letters in front of them. Direct students to move their frogs from letter to letter. As each student's frog touches a letter, have him say the letter's sound. Remind students that two *e*'s together make

a long /e/ sound. Write the word *free* on the board. Guide students to make more *fr* words, such as *frame, fresh, froze, from, frost,* and *fry*. At the end of the lesson, ask, "What sounds do you hear in the blend *fr*?" Reinforce the concept by reading a book from the *Frog and Toad* series by Arnold Lobel (Alfred A. Knopf) and having students wave their frog puppets in the air when they hear the word *frog* or another word with the *fr* blend.

Stop Signs

Do not let students stop working on blends! Copy the octagon pattern from the Blend Buddies reproducible (page 72) on red paper for each student. Write the word *stop* on the board. Draw a line under the *st* in the word *stop*. Tell students that *st* is a consonant blend. Say the word *stop* as you track the print. Have students use the letter cards from the Consonant Blends reproducible (page 70) to make *st* words, such as *step, stamp, stand, state, steal, steam,* and *stem*. Tell students to cut out the red octagons as you ask what sign is shaped the same way. Have each student write *stop* in the center of the pattern, then add other *st* words. Review the *st* blend by reading a book with many instances of the *st* blend, such as *Stop, Train, Stop!: A Thomas the Tank Engine Story* by Reverend Wilbert Awdry (Random House, 1995) and asking students to hold up their stop signs when they hear a word that begins with the *st* blend.

Blend Buddies

Cut out the patterns. Listen to
your teacher tell you how to use them.

First-Rate Reading™: Phonemic Awareness and Phonics • CD-104018 • © Carson-Dellosa
Basics

Sweeping Blends

Sweep the cobwebs from students' understanding of blends. Write the word *sweep* on the board. Draw a line under the *sw* in the word *sweep*. If students have completed several consonant blend lessons, ask a volunteer to identify the blend in the word *sweep*. Say the word as you track the print. Give each student a dry paintbrush to use as a broom. Have students use the letter cards from the Consonant Blends reproducible (page 70) and place the cards *s*, *w*, *i*, and *m* in front of them. Then, tell students to sweep their paintbrushes under each letter to help them sweep the sounds together to make a word. Ask, "What word does *s*, *w*, *i*, *m* spell?" Write *swim* on the board. Guide students to make the words *swine*, *swing*, *swan*, *sweet*, and *swell* with their letter cards and "brooms." Write each word on the board as students read it. Review the words at the end of the lesson. As a special treat, have students *swap* (return to you) their paintbrushes for *sweets* (pieces of candy).

Snake Sounds

Have a volunteer review what you have taught about consonant blends, including blends students have already learned. Write the word *snake* on the board. Draw a line under the *sn* in the word *snake*. Ask a volunteer to identify the consonant blend in the word. Let the volunteer stand near the board, say the word, and track the print. Give each student a copy of the Snake Sounds reproducible (page 74) and instruct her to cut out the tongues. Direct her to cut the slits on the head of the snake and slide the first tongue through the slits so that the *a*, *k*, and *e* are next to the *sn*. Ask, "How do you read the letters *s*, *n*, *a*, *k*, *e*?" Work with students to pull the tongues through the slits and read the rest of the *sn* words. Next, cut a large snake shape out of bulletin board paper that is the length of a bulletin board. Tape the snake to a wall and use a marker to divide it into segments. Have each student take a turn writing one *sn* word in a segment.

Blend Buddies

On yellow index cards, write the *bl*, *cl*, and *fl* blends on the far right sides of the cards. Write each blend five times, then write each of the following rimes on another color of index card: *-ack*, *-ame*, *-aim*, *-ast*, *-end*, *-ue*, *-ue*, *-am*, *-ap*, *-ap*, *-ean*, *-ip*, *-ip*, *-at*, *-op*. Write the rimes text on the far left side of each card. Have students find their "Blend Buddies." Give half of the students a blend card and the other half a rime card, making sure to distribute a match for each card. When you say "Blend Buddies," have students find "Blend Buddies" to put blend and rime cards together to make words. If students match two cards that make a real word, then they have found their "Blend Buddies." If the cards do not make a word, students should look for other possible matches. (Students will have more than one possible buddy.) Be available to tell students if their words are real words, and explain that some real words sound like the words they have made but are spelled differently. If students find "Blend Buddies" right away, have both of them write the word and then try to write sentences using the word while waiting for the other students to find their "Blend Buddies." Finally, repeat and let students make new words.

Name _____

Snake Sounds

Cut out the strips of paper. Cut the slits. Weave each strip through the slits to make words.

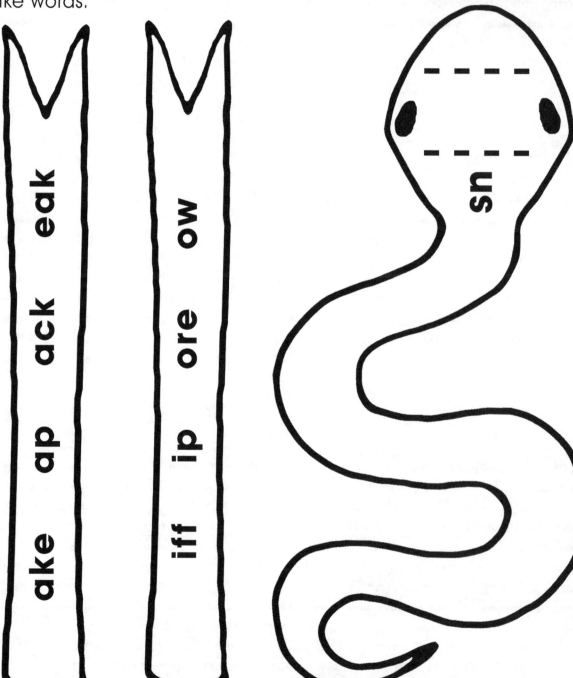

eak

ack

ap

ake

ow

ore

ip

iff

us

First-Rate Reading™: Phonemic Awareness and Phonics Basics • CD-104018 • © Carson-Dellosa

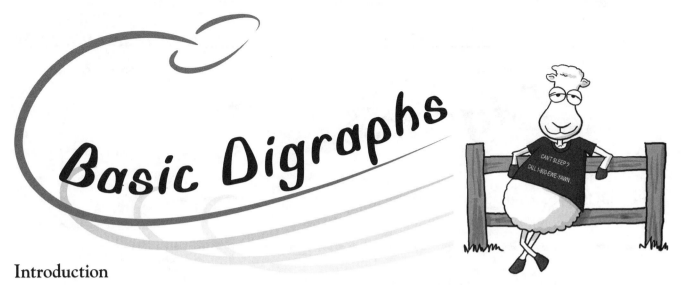

Basic Digraphs

Introduction

Students are usually taught to recognize the digraphs *ch*, *sh*, and *th* first, and learn *ph* later since it is less common. When students recognize these letter combinations, they will learn to read many new words with ease.

Counting Sheep

Review students' knowledge of blends, then explain that blends are not digraphs because in blends, the two consonants together still make two sounds. Tell students that when two consonants that are next to each other make one sound, they are called *digraphs*. Write the word *sheep* on the board. Draw a line under the letters *sh*. Have students say the sounds that the individual letters *s* and *h* usually make. Then, tell students that when *s* and *h* are together in a word, they make the /sh/ sound. Say the word *sheep* as you track the print. Give each student a copy of the Digraphs reproducible (page 76). Have students cut apart the letter cards, find the letters *s*, *h*, *e*, *e*, and *p*, and store the remaining letters in resealable, plastic bags. Have students run their fingers under the letters as they pronounce the word. (Remind students that *ee* sounds like long /e/). Help students use their letter cards to make the words *she*, *shut*, *ship*, *shade*, *shop*, and *shape*. Write the words on the board as students decode them, then give each student a copy of the Counting Sheep reproducible (page 77). Point out that the sheep are jumping over fences. Encourage students to use their letter cards to make new *sh* words and write *sh* words on the fences. Allow students to glue cotton balls to the sheep when they are finished writing. When the glue is dry, have each student remove some of the cotton from one of his sheep. Then, explain that students have *sh*eared their *sh*eep!

Digraph Shirts

Send notes to ask families to provide plain, white T-shirts. Repeat that when two consonants are next to each other and make one sound, they are called *digraphs*. Write *shirt* on the board. Underline the letters *sh*. Remind students that when *s* and *h* are together in a word, they make the /sh/ sound. Say *shirt* as you track the print. Have students use their letter cards from the Digraphs reproducible (page 76) to build *sheet*, *shed*, *shelf*, and *shock*. Write the words on the board as students decode them. Explain that digraphs can be at the ends of words, too. Write the word *wish* on the board. Underline the letters *sh*. Pronounce the word, then guide students to build *fish*, *dish*, *push*, and *rush*. Write the words on the board. Finally, give each student a T-shirt and a permanent marker. Tell students to write as many *sh* words as they can on their shirts, then let them read each other's "shirt words." Celebrate "Shirt Day" with *sh*erbet, candy *fish*, pasta *sh*ells and cheese, *sh*ortcake, *sh*ortbread, etc. (Get family permission and check for allergies and religious or other food preferences before completing the food portion of this activity.)

Name _____

Digraphs

Cut apart the cards. Use them to make words.

a	b	c	d	e	e
f	h	i	k	l	m
n	o	p	r	s	t
t	u	w	y		

First-Rate Reading™: Phonemic Awareness and Phonics Basics • CD-104018 • © Carson-Dellosa

Counting Sheep

On each fence, write letters to
make a word that begins with the digraph *sh*.

Shoe Shine

Review digraphs and the fact that when *s* and *h* are together in a word, they make the /sh/ sound as in the word *shoe*. Have students brainstorm other words that begin and end with the digraph *sh*. Write students' suggestions on the board and add the words *bush, crash, dash, leash,* and *trash*. Give each student a piece of white construction paper, a pencil, and scissors. Direct students to stand on the paper as their classmates trace their shoes. Have each student write at least four words that contain *sh* on her shoe prints, then cut out the paper shoe prints. Display the shoe prints on a bulletin board titled "We're in Step with Digraphs!"

Chocolate Words

Use this favorite sweet to teach the *ch* digraph. Explain that when *c* and *h* are together in a word, they make the /ch/ sound as in the word *chocolate*. Have the class repeat the word. Have students use the letter cards from the Digraphs reproducible (page 76) to make the words *chat, chin, chip, chop, chase,* and *cheap*. Give each student a piece of light brown construction paper and have him use a marker to divide his paper into 12 sections. Direct each student to write a *ch* word in each section of the "chocolate bar." Have students cut out the chocolate bars and share the *ch* words. To reward students, allow them to eat small pieces of chocolate. (Before distributing chocolate, ask families for permission and inquire about students' food allergies and religious or other preferences.)

Say Cheese!

Review the *ch* digraph. Write the word *cheese* on the board. Draw a line under the letters *ch* and say the /ch/ sound and the word *cheese* with students. Track the print as you say the word. Have students use the letter cards from the Digraphs reproducible (page 76) to make the words *chime, chose, chum,* and *chunk*. (To vary the activity, let students make the words using alphabet-shaped cereal or pasta, magnetic letters, or letter tiles). Explain that some words end in *ch*. Guide students to make the words *each, teach, reach,* and *beach*. Give each student three brown construction paper circles and three yellow sticky notes. Have students stick the yellow sticky notes to the circles to look like cheese on burgers. Direct students to write a *ch* word on each note. Post the cheeseburgers on a bulletin board titled "Say Cheese!" If time permits, allow students to draw or cut out and display other foods that contain the *ch* digraph, such as chewing gum, chocolate, chips, sandwich, etc.

Chain of Words

Give each student a long piece of green construction paper (approximately 12" x 1" or 30.5 cm x 2.5 cm) and a piece of string. Have each student add eyes and other facial features to the top of one end of the paper. Review the *ch* digraph and the fact that *ch* can be found at the ends of words. Write the word *inch* on the board. Draw a line under the letters *ch* and say the word as you track the print. Have students use the letter cards from the Digraphs reproducible (page 76) to build the words *inch, much, peach, pinch, ranch, rich,* and *such.* Then, have students explore the classroom—inch by inch! Let each student pretend to make her inchworm crawl around the classroom to find a word that contains the *ch* digraph. Demonstrate how an inchworm crawls, if necessary. When students find their words, have them hang the inchworms near the words by taping the worms to string and taping the other end of the string near the word. After students leave for the day, rearrange the worms, placing them near other *ch* words. The following morning, let students find their worms and identify the *ch* words near them.

Thumb Prints

Show how learning the *th* digraph can make students feel as if they are "all thumbs." Review what students have learned about digraphs, then introduce a new digraph. Tell the class that when *t* and *h* are together in a word, they make the /th/ sound. (Note: there is a difference between voiced and nonvoiced *th*. When students touch their throats and say words like *the, this, than,* etc., they should feel a vibration as they say the /th/. This is voiced *th*. When students say nonvoiced *th*-words like *thief, thank, thought,* etc., they will only feel the vibration as they start saying the vowel sounds in the words.) Say the word *thumb* for students. Have students brainstorm other words that start with the /th/ sound, such as *thank, thick, thief, than, thin, thing, think, third, the, that, them, then, this,* and *three.* Write the words on the board. Tell students that sometimes the /th/ sound comes at the end of a word. Add the words *bath, math, path,* and *tooth* to the list. Challenge each student to write a sentence using as many *th* words as possible, then have students illustrate their sentences using thumbprints. Give every three students an ink pad to share. Have students press their thumbs into the ink and then on the paper. Direct students to add details to the thumbprints (such as eyes, legs, hats, etc.) with markers. Assemble the sentences into a class book titled *Thumb Through Our TH Book!*

Words in My Mouth

Give each student a white paper plate. Review what students have learned about the *th* digraph. Write the word *mouth* on the board. Draw a line under the letters *th*. Tell the class that when *t* and *h* are together, they make the /th/ sound. Say the word *mouth* as you track the print. Have students use the letter cards from the Digraphs reproducible (page 76) to make the words *south*, *cloth*, *moth*, *teeth*, and *with*. Have each student fold her paper plate in half to form a "mouth." Direct students to write *th* words in the *mouth* and add details, such as eyes, teeth, lips, and a tongue. Have each student hold her folded plate in one hand and open and close her hand to make the mouth "say" *th* words.

Thumpety Thump Thump

Use a noisy activity to catch students' attention and reinforce knowledge of the *th* digraph. Make a fist and gently thump it on a desk. Ask students to guess what sound that makes. Guide students to think of a sound word that starts with the *th* digraph. Share that *thump* is the sound word you are looking for. Choose a children's book with several instances of the *th* digraph, such as *Where the Wild Things Are* by Maurice Sendak (HarperCollins, 1963). As you read the book aloud, encourage students to gently thump on their desks with their fists whenever they hear a word with the *th* digraph, such as *thing*, *the*, *anything*, etc. Each time you hear a thump, ask a volunteer to repeat the *th* word, and write it on the board. Repeat with other children's books, if desired, to create a word wall of *th* words.

Telephone Phun

If students have mastered *ch*, *sh*, and *th* digraphs, introduce the *ph* digraph. Sit at your desk or with students in a circle. Pretend to dial a number on an imaginary phone. Instruct a student to pretend to answer. Ask the student, "What is a digraph?" If he does not answer correctly, "call" other volunteers until someone responds correctly. Then, call another student who is a good speller and ask her to guess what new digraph you are introducing. Give her a hint by telling her that this digraph is in the word *digraph* and also in the word *phone*. If necessary, write the words on the board and underline the *ph*. Ask students to call out other words with the *ph* digraph, such as *phrase*, *graph*, *alphabet*, *Phillip*, etc. List the words on the board and review their meanings. Pair students. Have students pretend to call each other and have short conversations using as many of these words as possible.